Plane Tales of the Skies

Plane Tales of the Skies

The experiences of pilots over
the Western Front during

the Great War

Wilfred Theodore Blake

LEONAUR

Plane Tales of the Skies
The experiences of pilots over
the Western Front during
the Great War

by Wilfred Theodore Blake

First published under the title
Plane Tales of the Skies

Leonaur is an imprint
of Oakpast Ltd

ISBN: 978-1-84677-958-9 (hardcover)
ISBN: 978-1-84677-957-2 (softcover)

http://www.leonaur.com

Contents

To A. G. B.

AND

THE OTHER INHABITANTS

OF "THE RUINS,"

ABOUKIR, EGYPT,

APRIL—JULY, 1917,

Introduction

The series of tales and sketches which make up this book are all founded on fact and are the actual experiences of pilots and observers, chiefly on the Western front.

Many of the stories will be identified by people connected with the Royal Air Force and the chief actors easily recognised. I regret that, for obvious reasons, their names cannot be given.

The book was practically completed before the formation of the Royal Air Force, so that the title of the old Royal Flying Corps has been retained in most cases. By the time this appears in print the amalgamation of the R.N.A.S. and R.F.C. should be complete, and sailors and soldiers alike settling down to the new order of things under the common title of "Airmen." To old members of the Force this is but a return to old times, for the large majority of the first two thousand pilots were trained at the Central Flying School when it was a joint naval and military school, under the command of a naval officer.

I wish to acknowledge the permission granted by Messrs. Hulton to republish certain of these tales which have previously appeared in their periodicals.

W. T. B.

Leamington
25—6—18

1

V.C.s of the Air

Since August, 1914, no fewer than twelve Victoria Crosses have been won by officers and men of the Royal Flying Corps, previous to the formation of the Royal Air Force. Of these one was gained by a N.C.O., the others by commissioned officers. In addition three of those who have won the V.C. have also been awarded the D.S.O. and M.C., whilst Major McCudden received the M.M. before he was awarded a commission.

The first officer to win the Victoria Cross was 2nd Lieutenant Rhodes Moorhouse, who received the honour on 22nd May, 1915. On April 26th of that year this officer was ordered to fly to Courtrai and bomb the station and railway there. To those accustomed to present-day work in the air this may not sound a very difficult order to obey, but when one realises the machines flown in those days, and the difficulties under which all flights were made, the affair assumes more serious proportions. The writer has vivid recollections of flying in the beginning of 1915.

Our best machines, probably of the B.E.2C type, were capable of flying about 75 miles an hour when in good condition. They were bad to fight from, slow in climb, and only capable of reaching about 12,000 feet. Some few aeroplanes were armed with the Lewis gun, which was then far from perfect and liable to many jams at critical moments. The bomb-dropping apparatus was of a most primitive type and acted occasionally, though it was impossible to drop bombs with anything like accuracy.

Engines were liable to "peter out" without much warning, and, lastly, the art of aerial manoeuvre was not then understood.

In spite of all these handicaps, Lieutenant Moorhouse set out to bomb a place some twenty-five miles behind the enemy's lines. He reached his objective, dropped his bombs, damaging the railway and station, and set out on the return. In order to place his shots accurately, he had descended to within a few hundred feet of the ground, and as he commenced to regain altitude he was badly hit from the machine-guns which fired on him from below.

His engine was also damaged, and he was unable to climb out of reach of danger. With blood pouring from his wounds and a groggy engine, he flew the journey home. Thirty-five miles of pain, fired at continually, fearing the machine might fall to pieces at any moment, he covered them, and reported the successful accomplishment of his mission. Then he fainted from pain and loss of blood, and soon expired in hospital.

The next officer to win the V.C. also died of the wounds he received in winning the decoration. Captain Liddell was severely wounded when carrying out a long reconnaissance, his right thigh being broken. The shock deprived him of consciousness for a time, during which the machine fell steadily earthwards out of control, the helpless observer meanwhile trying to revive the unconscious pilot. After a fall of nearly 3,000 feet, Captain Liddell regained consciousness and checked the fall of the aeroplane.

His control wheel was smashed; many wires were cut; holes appeared all over the planes; splintered ribs peered through the fabric; the under-carriage was shattered. It seems incredible that the pilot should have succeeded in bringing home his machine, and still more incredible that he landed without doing much more damage. For half an hour after he was wounded the pilot controlled the aeroplane, retaining his senses until he had safely crossed the lines and saved his observer's life. A month later he died of his wounds.

Captain Hawker, the next officer to win the distinction, is

still alive, and is not the famous aviator of pre-war days, but an officer of the Royal Engineers, and one of the very earliest members of the E. F.C. Even in the early days of July, 1915, he proved that one Englishman is worth three Germans by attacking three enemy machines at the then great altitude of nearly 12,000 feet.

Though only armed with the most primitive of guns and an automatic pistol, he drove off the first Hun, who fled for home and safety. Formation flying was unheard of then, or possibly Hawker might have had a rougher time with the three well-armed aeroplanes, all of which carried machine-guns and observers. The second German put up a tougher fight than his comrade, but was eventually sent to earth, out of control, with the engine damaged. The third and last was dealt with still more effectually, the pilot being killed at 10,000 feet, and the whole machine falling earthwards and crashing within our lines.

Looked at from the standard of today, this seems a very small affair for which to give the highest honour a soldier may receive, but when one pauses to reflect on the immense strides made in the air since that day, the combat assumes greater magnitude, and one realises the tremendous bravery of the man who would take on such odds, in an almost unknown element and with very much inferior weapons.

"For most conspicuous bravery, skill, and determination," reads the *Gazette* announcing the award of the V.C. to 2nd Lieutenant Insall. This was the last cross to be won in 1915, and even today the story of his achievement bears comparison with any which has since gained an officer the award "For Valour."

Lieutenant Insall was patrolling in a "Vickers Fighter," a primitive pusher aeroplane driven by a rotary engine which has long since gone out of date for service overseas. It may be of interest to note that this machine was the forerunner of the F.E.2b, the fighter which was evolved to combat the Fokker when the Germans were making their greatest bid for aerial domination. In this machine the pilot and his observer sighted an enemy when some way over the lines.

13

Insall promptly gave chase, and his Mechanic-Observer, Donald, awaited the opportunity to deal with his opponent. The Hun did not wait, but turned and fled. Gradually the British machine overtook the enemy, and in the excitement of the chase neither pilot nor observer noticed where the Hun was leading them. The first intimation they received that all was not well was when a terrific storm of shot burst around them. They had been entrapped into following their prey over a rocket battery, one of the most effective weapons against aircraft which existed at that time.

Despite the heavy fire which was brought to bear on them, Insall dived, got to close range, and enabled the observer to fire a drum of ammunition into the German machine, damaging its engine. The Hun dived through a low cloud, and another burst was fired, bringing him to earth in a field near Arras. Both Germans jumped out, dismounted their gun and turned it on the British machine. Insall thereupon dived, and Donald fired a fresh burst at the pair on the ground, who fled, one leaning heavily on the other, evidently wounded.

The sound of firing had brought up a body of troops, who opened fire on the aeroplane; but in spite of this the pilot turned, came even closer to the ground, and dropped an incendiary bomb on the wreckage of the German machine.

Having at last accomplished his work, he headed back for the lines, and as he was only about 2,000 feet from the ground and under heavy fire, put down the nose of the aeroplane in order to cross the trenches at a greater speed. A terrific bombardment was opened on them, to which Donald replied with the machine-gun. Unfortunately, before they could reach safety, a bullet pierced the petrol tank, and the engine at once commenced to splutter. However, they were safely over the lines and the pilot was able to choose a spot in which to land, which he did under the shelter of a wood about 500 yards behind the front trenches.

Although the machine might easily have been salved, Insall refused to leave it, and commenced to repair the damage. This, however, proved much more extensive than he had at first imagined, for the aeroplane was badly shot about and not at all in a fit condition to fly. In addition the Huns discovered his whereabouts, and commenced to shell the spot heavily.

Despite all these drawbacks—and the Huns put over some hundred and fifty shells—the machine was repaired during the night, and next day Insall flew the aeroplane home, with Donald as his passenger.

During 1916 only two V.C.s were awarded to the R.F.C., these being won by Captain Rees and Lieutenant Robinson.

Lieutenant Robinson's cross calls for comment in that, though not the first V.C. awarded for destroying a Zeppelin—which distinction goes to Lieutenant Warneford, of the R.N.A.S.—his was the first to be awarded to any person for action in England. The circumstances of the award are well known to everyone, and Robinson, as the first man to bring down a Zeppelin in England, was for some time a popular hero. He had been for some time serving in the "Zepp. strafing" Wing, and previously had frequently been employed as a ferry pilot. It is a fact worth noting that several other pilots who eventually won distinction for destroying airships were serving as ferry pilots, taking aeroplanes to France to replace casualties, at the same time, among them being Sowery, Tempest and Brandon, all of whom won the D.S.O. for the same reason that Robinson received the V.C.

The writer has recollections of their great use in taking over machines at the beginning of the Somme push, Brandon being a particularly hard-working pilot, during one period flying to France and returning by boat for a fresh machine no fewer than five times in one week. So far as I am aware, certainly up to the time when my connection with the ferry pilots ceased, the record in this direction was eight machines taken over in seven days.

On the day in which the pilot took over two machines, he was lucky enough to find an old aeroplane, which had done its time overseas, to fly back, this enabling him to do the double journey. Needless to say, this entails a great strain on the pilots who do the work, for they get very little sleep, and many suffer from sea-sickness daily when returning by boat across the Channel.

The only N.C.O. pilot who has won the V.C. is Sergeant Mottershead, whose gallantry in saving the life of his observer is worthy of the highest praise. Lieutenant Gower, the observer, escaped unharmed, but Mottershead lost his life from the terrible injuries he received. The writer heard the whole story from Lieutenant Gower whilst stationed with him shortly afterwards.

Whilst on patrol about 9,000 feet in a pusher fighter, Mottershead was attacked by a fast-flying German scout. Hopelessly outmanoeuvred, left standing for speed and flexibility, the pilot vainly tried to face his foe, so that the observer might use his gun to advantage. The combat was of short duration. A shot from the gun of the scout pierced the petrol tank, and the machine burst into flames. Satisfied with his work, the German pilot retired.

Imagine the plight of the pilot and observer 9,000 feet in the air with the aeroplane a roaring mass of flames. The chance of reaching the ground intact was very remote, a contingency hardly to be thought of. Yet, instead of giving up hope and letting things go, this very gallant man did his utmost to save the machine and his officer.

As the aeroplane was a pusher, in which type pilot and observer sat in front of the engine, the wind blew the flames away from their bodies, the pilot being the closer of the two to the blaze. Whilst the flames were gradually eating into the structure of the machine, Gower seized the fire-extinguisher, which is always carried, and sprayed it over the pilot, who, despite the terrific heat eating into his back, put down the nose of the fighter and dived steeply to earth. Two questions presented themselves to the observer's mind with equal magnitude—Would the fire kill Mottershead before they reached earth? And would the flames eat through the wooden booms, causing the whole structure to fall to pieces before it could be landed?

Gradually they crept nearer and nearer the ground, the pilot growing fainter with pain every moment. Even when it seemed that they might possibly reach earth before the aeroplane collapsed, it seemed impossible that the pilot would be able to land in safety—the crash would probably kill both passengers.

But Mottershead's marvellous pluck and endurance did enable him to land, and not only did he land, but chose a good spot in which to come to rest. At the moment the fighter touched ground the fire finished its work, and the whole fabric collapsed, throwing Gower clear of the wreckage, but pinning Mottershead beneath it. Had it been possible to extricate him in time, probably his life would have been saved, but the observer lay unconscious, and it was some minutes before help arrived and he was taken from the burning mass.

Covered with burns from head to foot, Mottershead was taken to hospital, but his injuries were too severe, and he died before the V.C. had been awarded.

Lieutenant Gower, not content with this experience, is again overseas, though in another theatre of operations.

The next V.C. to be awarded was that given to Captain Ball— probably the. most popular hero of the war, now unfortunately gone to bear company the other wearers of the bronze cross who have given their lives for their country. Ball's V.C. was not awarded for an isolated act of gallantry, but for consistent gallantry over a long period. Probably this is the first instance in which the highest honour has been awarded in this manner, though Bishop and McCudden are almost parallel cases.

Ball's career can only be described as meteoric. One day unheard of, for a few days the idol of the world, then a name only, to be remembered and held up to a future body of airmen as a pattern for them to follow. He received the Military Cross in July, 1916, the Distinguished Service Order in September, 1916, the bar to the D.S.O. in the same month, and a second bar in November of the same year. He also received the Russian Order of St. George in September, 1916. In June, 1917, he reached the culminating point, and received the Victoria Cross "for most conspicuous and consistent bravery from April 25th to May 6th, during which period Captain Ball took part in twenty-six combats in the air and destroyed eleven hostile aeroplanes, drove down two out of control, and forced several others to land." At this time Ball had destroyed forty-three aeroplanes and one balloon.

The official account of his first deed to win the D.S.O. is as follows:

"For conspicuous gallantry and skill. Observing seven enemy machines in formation, he immediately attacked one of them and shot it down at fifteen yards' range. The remaining machines retired. Immediately afterwards, seeing five more hostile machines, he attacked one at about ten yards' range and shot it down, flames coming out of the fuselage. He then attacked another of the machines, which had been firing at him, and shot it down into a village, where it landed on the top of a house. He then went to the nearest aerodrome for more ammunition, and, returning, attacked three more machines, causing them to dive under control. Being then short of petrol, he came home. His own machine was badly shot about in these fights."

Imagine the coolness of the pilot reserving his fire to be sure of hitting the target until he had closed to ten and fifteen yards' range, and the gluttony for aerial combat that prompted him, after already having destroyed three machines, to return to the nearest aerodrome for more ammunition. Such deeds seem scarcely human.

His death was recorded with terse brevity in the official *communiqué*: "Captain Albert Ball failed to return from this patrol." That was all.

Captain Bishop—"the Canadian Ball"—is another wearer of three distinctions,[1] and but for a curious stroke of bad luck he would probably have been the first to achieve this fame.

Whilst the writer was at Netheravon in the latter part of 1915, Bishop was sent down to train as an observer. He at once acquired a certain amount of local celebrity by reason of his indignation at not being allowed to become a pilot. Someone in authority had decided that he had not the requisite qualities

---

1. Now four, since the award of the D.F.O. 14

18

to fly: either his nerves were not quite good enough or he had not enough "go" in him, or some other fault was found. The observer's course, with its hours of wireless and photography, bored him; the only hours which aroused his enthusiasm were those devoted to gunnery.

All his spare time was spent on the ranges or in the gun-room, and by the time he had finished his course he was probably the best aerial shot on the station. Eventually he left for overseas with his squadron, still breathing out curses on those who condemned him to go as a passenger instead of piloting his own machine. He intended to apply again for permission to take his ticket and graduate as a pilot, and he amused us all by telling how, when his chance arrived, he would show them the mistake they had made. Even in those days he was fully confident of winning the V.C. when the time came.

It is highly probable that those days overseas as an observer were of great use to Bishop afterwards. He was able to perfect his gunnery and observe the habits and tactics of the Huns. This knowledge he afterwards turned to good account, being, in addition to a finished pilot, skilled in all the tricks of the air, a marvellous shot, who reserved his fire until sure of hitting the target and securing a victim.

He was first heard of by the public when he won the Military Cross at the end of May, 1917. Before the end of the year he had added to it both the D.S.O. and the V.C.

It is worthless to select any particular incident from his career for mention. His life overseas was filled with fighting from morning to night. Dull days were of no use to him. If he could not fight with machines in the air, he was happy worrying the infantry in the trenches or firing at the German mechanics at work in the hangars, or even chasing German Staff cars down the roads.

Luckily he is still alive and at work imparting his marvellous knowledge of gunnery to those who hope to emulate his feats in the air.

The third of the great trio is Major McCudden.

Joining the R.F.C. as a mechanic, McCudden soon took up flying, and as a N.C.O. pilot won the Military Medal at the end of 1916.

After he received his commission, he quickly made his way to the front rank of fighting pilots. M.C., D.S.O., bar to the D.S.O., and V.C. followed each other with such startling rapidity that flying folk were wondering what other honours he hoped to obtain. His death in July, 1918, through an accident, was a great loss to the Service.

McCudden, like Ball and Bishop, was an excellent shot, and a glutton for fighting. The following typical day's work shows the stuff of which such men are made.

At a few minutes to ten, McCudden left his aerodrome and crossed the trenches. By 10.30 he was over German territory and had sighted an enemy machine. Ten minutes later it had been shot down, and the British pilot was in full chase after another machine. At ten minutes to eleven this became a blazing wreck. A few minutes later a Hun had the temerity to attack, but after a short conflict, in which McCudden's radiator was damaged, the Hun fled earthwards.

Owing to the damage done to his engine, McCudden returned to the aerodrome, shooting down another enemy on his way home. Having safely landed, instead of resting, he promptly took another machine, and at a few minutes after twelve was again looking for Huns. He did not have to seek long, and another combat ensued. This was of greater duration than the others, but ended in the usual way, the German aeroplane diving to earth a blazing wreck. After this McCudden went home to lunch.

Four machines destroyed and another driven to earth is not a bad morning's work for the best of pilots.

The latest recipients of the V.C. are Lieutenant A. Jerrard and 2nd Lieutenant McCleod, both of whose awards were gazetted on May 1st, the day on which the Royal Air Force was formed. These officers were therefore the first of the R.A.F. to be decorated.

Jerrard, who died of his injuries, was a short time ago undergoing instruction at an aerodrome near the East Coast, and whilst there was regarded as such a reckless pilot that for a time his instruction was stopped, as it was feared that he would one day break his neck. He was one of the most daring pilots the writer has ever known, and even before he graduated practised aerobatics which were usually only performed by the most expert and experienced pilots. He was absolutely reckless and devoid of fear, a most dangerous man to have on a training aerodrome, but a most useful pilot to employ overseas.

He won his V.C. in the following manner:

Whilst on an offensive patrol with two other officers, he attacked five enemy machines, shooting one down in flames, and following it to within a hundred feet of the earth.

He then proceeded to a neighbouring aerodrome, and from the height of only fifty feet proceeded to attack it single-handed. To commence with, he took on some nineteen machines, sending one crashing to the ground. He then returned to help another aeroplane of the patrol which was in difficulties, and destroyed a third machine.

Fresh numbers of German machines put off to attack him, and he fought them one after the other, singly and in groups. At last, wounded and weary, he was overwhelmed by the enormous number of foes and driven to the ground.

McCleod's V.C. recalls the circumstances of Mottershead's gallant death, though in this case the pilot lived through the ordeal.

Whilst flying at a height of 5,000 feet, McCleod and his observer were attacked by eight enemy triplanes. Three of these were shot down, and McCleod was wounded five times. Then the petrol tank was pierced and the aeroplane burst into flames.

Despite his wounds, the pilot climbed from his seat, stood on the plane, and from this position controlled the machine, side-slipping it earthwards, so that the flames blew away from his observer, who had been hit six times. All the time the remaining Huns kept up the attack and the observer fired at them through the flames of the burning machine.

The aeroplane crashed in No Man's Land, and McCleod proceeded to drag the observer clear of the wreckage, being meanwhile fired on from the trenches. He eventually put his companion in a position of comparative safety, and was then again wounded by a bomb, having just sufficient strength left to roll into a shell hole, from which he was rescued later.

Deeds such as these hardly seem performed by mere mortals, and form the best argument against those who urge that we are a degenerate race.

2

"Pull Her up, Sir!"

As the autumn mists began to clear before the sun the two fighting aeroplanes left their aerodrome and crossed the line. The clouds were low and broken, and both machines flew together, just away below the lowest fleecy layer, waiting until the mists should clear before mounting to a higher altitude and looking for a German machine to attack.

This time, however, the two pilots were taken unawares, for out of a gap in the clouds shot two Albatross scouts, pouring streams of bullets from their guns. The pilot of the lower scout, unfortunately for himself, overshot his target, and before he could manoeuvre his machine into safety the British fighter came round into position, and the waiting gunner pumped burst after burst into his enemy. For one sickening moment the Albatross wavered and seemed to hesitate, as though the pilot was uncertain whether to try and return to the attack or fly for home and safety; and then the whole aeroplane seemed to burst into flames, and dropped burning to the ground.

Meanwhile things had not gone so well for the other British fighter. The scout which followed in the wake of its doomed fellow was more cautiously handled, and the pilot, instead of continuing his wild dive, pulled up his machine, swerved to the right, and attacked the slower machine from the side. Almost at once his shots took effect. A bullet passed through the petrol tank, and was deflected into the pilot's back, wounding him seriously. Notwithstanding the pain, the pilot retained his consciousness of the position, swung round the fighter, and charged straight at the attacking scout. The observer waited his opportunity, and when a collision seemed imminent pressed the trigger of his gun. Streaks of flame shot forward, and a stream of lead played around the German aeroplane. The scout pilot pushed up the nose of his machine to avoid contact with the madly-charging fighter, but when at the top of the zoom, the Albatross did not flatten out, relapsed into a tail-slide, side-slipped, and spun furiously to earth.

The pilot turned painfully in his seat and grinned weakly at the mechanic-gunner. Then the pain overcame him, he fell forward in his seat, and fainted away.

Bereft of a guiding hand the aeroplane put her nose down and commenced to spin rapidly. Only a few thousand feet remained for them to fall, and the observer, thinking that possibly the pilot was merely muddled through loss of blood, leaned forward and tapped him on the shoulder to try and waken him. Finding his efforts of no avail, he stood up in his seat. The pilot had fainted with the stick jammed between his legs. Only one thing could be done to save them—the pilot must be moved and the stick pushed forward to bring the machine again under control. To do this the observer would have to climb out of his seat and walk to the pilot's cockpit.

As the observer realised that this was the only course he could pursue he shrank from the ordeal. To climb along the plane of a machine flying level in mid-air was sufficiently bad, but attempting it with the aeroplane diving through space and spinning madly as well seemed an impossible undertaking Little time was left for consideration. In a very few minutes the aeroplane would crash, and all efforts would be too late. Cautiously he stepped out of his seat, carefully choosing the side where the wind-pressure would hold him against the fuselage. Inch by inch he crept along the plane until the pilot's cockpit was reached. Then, leaning over and holding on with one hand, he pulled the pilot back, and pushed the stick forward. Almost at once the spin ceased, but the dive still continued.

Then the pilot's eyes opened. Either the change of motion or the alteration of position brought him to, and he recovered his faculties just enough to obey his observer's instructions.

Mechanically he brought the machine into flying position, and held her there, for there was yet some way to go, as they were still over enemy territory. Minute after minute went by, and still the aeroplane held her course, swaying and rocking like a drunken man.

At last the trenches were passed, and machine-gun fire from below ceased. In a short while it would be possible to land in comparative safety. But at this juncture the pilot fainted away again, and the machine sank earthwards. The observer shook him by the shoulder, and shouted to him, but he was too far gone to hear.

In front of the machine loomed a field. The observer knew that on the far side of it an aerodrome existed. Desperately he leaned forward again, and shook the pilot. "Pull her up, sir!" he shouted. "Pull her up!"

Something touched the pilot's befogged brain, and without opening his eyes he pulled the stick in towards him. The aeroplane shot upwards, clearing the hedge by inches.

Then the observer saw the level stretch of the landing-ground, and obtained a firmer grip of the machine so that he should not be thrown off by the shock of landing. He was frozen by the cold in his exposed position, but, having brought the pilot so far, would not now give up.

Down sank the nose of the aeroplane in the slack grip of the pilot's unconscious hands, and once more the observer exhorted him to "Pull her up, sir!" Again the pilot obeyed, and as the wheels touched ground the observer switched off the engine. Up shot the machine for a few feet, then, bereft of any motive power, pancaked to earth. A crackling noise betrayed the fracture of the undercarriage, and the aeroplane stopped.

Then the ambulance moved over to them.

3

Bombing the Boche

This is the tale of twelve machines which set out to bomb the Boche.

Each machine carried one huge bomb, the senior officer carrying four smaller ones in addition. Orders had not been issued for a concerted raid; everything was left to the discretion of the individual pilots, who were expected to lay their eggs where they were calculated to do most damage and annoy the Hun in the highest degree. In fact each officer had a roving commission. What more could be desired by youth searching for adventure?

One by one the bombing aeroplanes left the ground, laden with freights of high explosive carried under the pilot's seat, circled for height, and vanished towards the lines. Last of all the Flight Commander left, his machine climbing slowly on account of the extra weight carried.

The first pilot to cross the trenches was not very ambitious. He had been in France many months and was tired. Whilst a hard worker, he was not given to spectacular displays; rather he believed in getting his work done and not running after trouble. That would arrive in its own time. Accordingly he selected the railway line midway between two important towns for his attention, planed down to within five hundred feet of the earth, and released two hundred and thirty pounds of high explosive on the centre of the permanent way. A terrific explosion, which caused the aeroplane to stagger, resulted. When the smoke had cleared away he saw a huge hole with masses of tangled iron where the track had run. Satisfied, he returned unmolested to the aerodrome.

Three of the pilots had selected the same mark for their bombs, with the result that a certain town suffered severely that morning, the station being disorganised for some days after. Also it was reported that the German headquarters had a narrow escape, and many casualties occurred in a part of the town crowded with enemy troops.

The pilot of the fifth machine, being an adventurous soul, young and enthusiastic, roamed over the country looking for a good target. He had no plan in his head, but just waited for something to turn up. At last he saw an objective, which seemed worthwhile, a long train moving slowly up towards the line. He descended to make a closer inspection, satisfied himself that it was packed with troops, and dropped his bomb, neatly severing the creeping train. One truck seemed to leap bodily into the air, several were overturned, while the rest telescoped one into the other.

Next the pilot dived at the engine, pouring out a rain of bullets upon the driver, who leaped from the footplate and ran for safety. Scores of troops jumped from the damaged carriages and dashed for the shelter of a neighbouring wood. On these the pilot next turned his gun, causing many casualties before the trees hid them from sight, enabling them to open fire upon the aeroplane.

Unable to do further damage in that spot, he left reluctantly, and, having no more bombs to drop, flew towards home.

More excitement was, however, in store for him, for before he reached the lines an Albatross scout dived out of the clouds, firing as it fell. He banked steeply, zoomed, and then followed on the tail of the Hun.

Unfortunately his machine was not designed for fighting purposes, and the faster scout outdistanced him, giving up the combat, evidently thinking that "he who fights and runs away" applied equally to aerial warfare as to terrestrial battles.

Numbers six and seven pilots kept company, dropping their

eggs on a large munition dump. It was unfortunate in one way that the first bomb missed the target, merely blowing a hole in an already shell-pocked field, but in reality it turned out a very good thing, for as the second machine flew up wind to deposit its load of explosives where the first bomb should have settled, a German fighter appeared on the scene, the anti-aircraft fire, which had been of the usual intensity, ceased, and things looked ugly for the heavily-weighted aeroplane.

Fortunately the pilot who had dropped his bomb without success awaited the result of his companion's effort, and on the arrival of the Hun dashed at him, occupied his attention until a roar from below with a huge sheet of flame proclaimed the fact that the dump was hit, and then manoeuvred the Hun so that both British machines could attack. A minute later the planes of the fighter collapsed, the wreckage tumbling to earth in a shapeless mass as its victors left for home.

Two other aeroplanes, though not acting together, reached a railway station about the same time, but both missed their objective, merely damaging the line before returning to roost.

The Flight Commander, who carried five bombs, enjoyed his day completely. He crossed the trenches at a great height, ran into the clouds, and when he emerged was unable to discover his whereabouts. Seeing a station far below, he descended, hoping to be able to read the name of the place on the platform. When about a hundred feet above ground he accomplished his object, and then noticed a train in the siding. Deeming it a suitable target, he dropped one of the smaller bombs as a souvenir, following it with another on an adjacent shed which he judged contained ammunition. The resulting explosion proved his surmise to be correct.

Sometime later he again encountered a railway station, and thinking that stations brought him luck, descended to reconnoitre. Alongside the platform a train was drawn up, its many trucks laden with pit-props destined for the trenches. As this seemed a most favourable target he steadied his machine and dropped the two hundred and thirty pounds of explosive. A fair hit was secured. A deafening roar reached the ears of the pilot as two trucks left the rails, ascending perpendicularly into the air. Others were overturned, the permanent way was torn up, and the buildings badly damaged.

Before leaving that spot the pilot decided to drop his remaining missiles. He accordingly flew low over the siding and released both bombs over a shunting train. This time his luck deserted him; one bomb burst close by the train, but not close enough to do any damage; the other failed to explode.

Having finished his work he went home.

On arriving he found that ten machines had already returned, and one was yet awaited. Only one of the ten had passed a blank day, the engine showing signs of trouble, and making the pilot wisely decide to go back to the aerodrome rather than risk a landing on the other side of the lines.

The eleven pilots stood in a little group awaiting the return of the last of their flock.

He was already overdue, being one of the first to leave, and his petrol would not carry him much longer.

The C.O. appeared on the scene and looked at his watch.

"Give him another quarter of an hour," he observed.

Slowly the minutes passed, and slighter grew the chances of the missing pilot's return.

At last the C.O. turned away

"Afraid it's no use waiting," he said. "Poor beggar!"

Gradually the knot of people dispersed, and the officers walked soberly towards the mess, where others were already occupied with their meal.

As the C.O. seated himself an orderly appeared, handing him the pink slip of a field telegram.

He read it and his face relaxed.

Lieutenant —— in machine No. ——, landed here at 0830. Machine badly shot about. Pilot unhurt.

was the message which had brought relief.

4

Three O'Clock in the Morning Courage

Three o'clock in the morning is a horrible time to be awakened, and when in addition an order is received to get into the air as quickly as possible to attack raiding machines, it may well be imagined that the pilot concerned is not in the best of moods. Consequently the flight commander was not exactly whistling for joy when he reached the aerodrome a few minutes after he had been awakened.

After ascertaining that petrol and oil tanks were full, that the gun was working, a large supply of ammunition handy, and all controls in order, he ran up the engine and soon vanished in the greyness which was then overcoming the darkness of night.

His orders were rather vague. He had been told that enemy aircraft were bombing a large town behind our lines, and that he was to attack them. That was all, the method of attack was left to his own initiative.

Realising that by the time he reached the town the raiders would probably have departed, he decided to seek their aerodrome and await their return. With this object in view he flew west over the lines looking for the lights of the landing flares which he knew would be laid out to guide the returning squadron.

At last, through the greyness, he distinguished far below the pin-points of light which indicated the position of the enemy aerodrome. He moved back the throttle lever and planed slowly down in wide circles, seeking the returning aircraft, finally, when some three thousand feet from the ground taking up a position a few miles away from the landing place, between the home of the Huns and their late objective.

For some time he flew backwards and forwards across the route of the returning raiders without seeing any sign of activity. Then, at last, in the darkness he discerned a darker spot which rapidly grew larger and nearer until he could distinguish it as an enemy aeroplane. It was a huge double-engined machine, flying at a higher altitude than himself, so he waited until it had passed, hoping to remain unnoticed in the darkness, then place himself under the enemy's tail and release a stream of lead from his gun.

Unfortunately for this design the German observer was keeping a good look out, and saw the British machine before the pilot got into position, and before the pilot could train his gun on the enemy the Hun commenced to fire, without, however, doing any damage.

Quickly adjusting his gun the pilot returned the fire, spraying the planes of the bomber with shots. No vital spot was hit as the range was long, but as the British fighter closed with his adversary his shots crept closer to the pilot's cockpit and petrol tank.

They were rapidly approaching the aerodrome, and the raider dropped its nose, diving for safety, breaking off the combat. The British pilot manoeuvred into position, took careful aim, and then the gun jammed.

In order to prevent the enemy landing, and thus reaching safety, he charged straight at the bomber, making the German pilot swerve off his course. Again the fighter charged at the Hun, again forcing the machine from its path. Time after time the manoeuvre was repeated until the aerodrome was passed and the British pilot had time to attend to his gun.

He soon rectified the jam and again poured a heavy fire into the enemy, meanwhile keeping in such a position that an effective sight could not be brought to bear on him.

Suddenly a red light flared out from the big bomber, and an answering signal appeared on the aerodrome behind them. Following the red light, fire from the ground was brought to bear on the British aeroplane. Machine guns and "flaming onions" played their part; bullets whistled through the planes; masses of blazing fire hurtled through the air; a very inferno seemed loosened.

When the pilot recovered from his first amazement he saw that the enemy had taken advantage of his temporary confusion, and was again making for the aerodrome. Once more the superior speed of the British machine was useful, and the pilot flew to cut off his unwilling adversary. Again he poured in a shower of bullets, forcing the German to turn from the homeward path.

He noticed that when he closed with the enemy the bombardment from below was discontinued. Probably the danger of setting the big bomber alight with "flaming onions" was too great to be disregarded. The pilot therefore kept close to his foe, seeking to kill the German as it seemed impossible to damage his engines.

At last he got a fair target and from the range of only a few yards poured in a long burst of fire. First he saw, in the now growing light of dawn, the observer slip forward in his seat. Then the pilot disappeared, and the machine dipped her nose, diving steeply as the dead body fell forward on the controls.

As the bomber crashed outside the aerodrome the bombardment from below opened with even greater intensity.

During the last stages of the fight the British machine had descended to within a thousand feet of the ground, and was now an easy target for the gunners on the aerodrome. Realising the danger, the pilot sped westward still farther into German territory until out of range from the aerodrome. Then the scout swung round and flew eastward towards the rising sun, towards home, rest, and breakfast.

5

In No Man's Land

Escort work is among the most exciting duties carried out by scout machines, and many fierce combats are fought by the pilots who place themselves between their convoy and the formation of attacking Huns. Sometimes the escort saves his flock and himself also; occasionally a shot-about machine controlled by a weary pilot, faint from pain and loss of blood, creeps into the aerodrome long after the others have landed. On one occasion a returning formation of bombers was about to cross the lines into safety when the rearmost scout saw several enemy aircraft hanging in the clouds about to attack. He dashed forward to place himself between them and their prey, compelling the Germans to alter their plan of attack, and fall upon him to destroy his machine before diving at the unprotected bombers. The British pilot did not refuse combat, but dashed at each foe in turn, D 39 herding them like a sheepdog, keeping them away from his charges.

Slowly the bombers vanished in the distance, leaving the escort alone with three of the enemy. Now, however, he was able to concentrate on one target, and, singling out his foe, attacked fiercely, driving him down lower and lower, firing bursts from his gun as opportunity offered. At last his shots went home, the machine burst into flames, broke into pieces and fell headlong to earth.

He then turned to deal with the others, who had been firing from long range during the last affair. As he flew towards them they thought better of it and vanished in the light clouds which hung overhead.

Having nothing further to wait for, the pilot steered for home, thinking of the rest before him, for this one job should end his day's work. Unfortunately he neglected to keep a sharp enough look out, and the first warning he had of the return of the two Germans was a blow on the right ankle which broke the bone. Almost at the same moment another bullet pierced the petrol tank, and the engine stopped.

He was now in a terrible position. Utterly unable to turn and attack the enemy, he was just as incapable of flying from them. The pain in his ankle was almost intolerable, petrol was pouring over him from the pierced tank. This might ignite at any moment, and death would be certain.

Ever hopeful, knowing that the trenches were only a short distance away, he put down the nose of his machine, commencing to glide to safety. Time and again he kicked the rudder-bar with his sound foot, causing the aeroplane to sway drunkenly from side to side, making it more difficult for the following pilots to place their shots accurately. Showers of lead played about him, almost every part of the machine was hit, but the pilot himself received no further injury.

He soon saw the trenches before him. Little by little he glided towards safety, losing height the while. Had he sufficient altitude to carry him to the British lines? If he managed to scrape over, the margin would be very fine. And all the time the bullets flew around him and the devilish "Rat-tat-tat-tat" of machine-guns sounded in his ears.

At last the trenches were below him, and safety seemed at hand. Hot rifle and machine-gun fire broke out from both sides, the British trying to drive off the attacking planes, the Germans trying to bring down the gliding machine before it reached safety.

Another few yards would have done it, but the badly damaged aeroplane could hold together no longer; a plane snapped off, and the wreckage dropped to earth between the lines. The fall had not been great, the pilot was not hurt again, and he quickly endeavoured to extricate himself from the mass of wires and splintered wood.

As he rose from the remains a cheer broke from the British lines, followed at once by heavy fire from the German trenches. Luck could last no longer. As the pilot stepped clear of the wreckage, painfully limping on his damaged leg, two more bullets found their mark, and he rolled over with his other leg broken, and a shattered arm.

With his remaining strength he rolled into a shell hole, gaining a few moments' respite from the heavy fire.

Meanwhile the two German scouts, who had not been driven off, seeing what happened, returned, dived at the wounded pilot, and opened fire as he lay helpless in the shell hole.

This proved too much for the Australians who manned the British trenches. A terrific fire was opened on the two German aeroplanes and machine-guns sprayed the opposite lines, whilst a party crawled up a sap near the head of which lay the wounded man. Awaiting their opportunity they dashed over the top, seized the helpless pilot, and returned to the trenches, bearing him with them. One of their number was left behind dead.

In this manner was the pilot brought back to safety.

6

Out of Line

Throughout the day things had gone wrong. First his engine had refused to start up, causing him to be late at the rendez-vous many thousand feet in the air; then the extreme cold and rarefied atmosphere at the tremendous height had caused it to splutter and fire weakly, with the result that the revolutions had dropped and he had fallen out of the formation.

He watched the others gradually draw farther and farther ahead as he tried every possible method to make the engine pick up. He did not mean to give in and return home if he could help it, but as he flew on over the enemy's country he gradually lost height and saw the formation growing smaller and smaller in the distance. He turned round and grimaced at his observer, who smiled and pointed dejectedly towards home. The pilot nodded, banked his machine, and swung her round, setting a course back to the aerodrome. Anyhow, the day's work would soon be finished, and that was something to be thankful for.

He retraced his path, gradually losing height the while, un-til the jagged line of trenches was nearly reached, when a new note crept into the roar of the engine. It was firing regularly and strongly; the revolution meter showed that all was well.

Again he looked round at his observer. That worthy grinned his appreciation of the new state of affairs and nodded assurance to the mute questioning of the pilot's face. Once more the ma-chine swung round and headed for enemy territory.

By now the formation was well out of sight, but both pilot

and observer knew their destination and the object of the raid. They had good maps and confidence in each other; the aeroplane was good when the engine was running well; they were armed and well seasoned, and had come safely through a good many raids and several combats—there seemed no reason why the day's work should not be continued, especially as "Archie" seemed abnormally quiet, and no suspicious specks were to be seen in the surrounding sky.

Green fields gradually grew more plentiful as the shell-pocked region of the trenches was left behind, roads became more clearly defined, and positions more easily placed on the map. The railway which acted as guide went straight through the heart of the country and led eventually to the aerodrome which was to be bombed.

When nearing their destination the pilot turned to see that his observer was prepared for eventualities. Not that he had any doubt in the matter, but it is as well not to neglect any precautions when in the neighbourhood of the Hun.

At last the rest of the formation was sighted returning, the long V trailing over the sky in regular order. Sundry puffs of smoke proclaimed that the gunners were busy below, but no hostile machines appeared to be attacking. The pilot passed close enough to wave to the last aeroplane as it passed, and then prepared to drop his bombs where they appeared to be most needed. The absence of the enemy tempted him down, and though "Archie" was strafing merrily it became an almost negligible quantity at that altitude.

Carefully adjusting his bomb-sight, he released the first missile. So low was he that he could hear the explosion, and a moment later flames spurted from the large hut which had been hit. His observer beamed with joy, and the next bomb crashed through the roof of a hangar which by the look of things had already received bad treatment that day.

By now machine-gun fire was being sprayed around from countless spots on the aerodrome, and the observer was busy trying to silence it with his Lewis gun. Bomb after bomb was dropped, but no aeroplane attempted to come out to the attack, and at last the pilot pushed up the nose of his machine and steered for home. He was in an excellent mood; all his bombs had been effective—indeed, how could he miss at that low altitude?—and he was longing to hear how the others had done, and why none of them had been molested.

In the midst of his thoughts he was recalled to immediate business by a sudden splutter of the engine. He glanced at the revolution meter—it was falling rapidly—and at last, with a final explosion from the engine, the needle dropped to zero.

As he watched the propeller stop he mechanically pushed down the nose of his machine, and realising in a flash that he must inevitably be captured, decided that the Hun aerodrome was as good a landing-place as any in the neighbourhood. He accordingly landed as far away from the hangars as possible, in order to give his observer every chance to do his share of the business.

That worthy was busy with a Very pistol, and as the aeroplane bumped to a standstill sprang out, and a moment later the machine was in flames. Neither of them had any papers of importance, so having done all they could they walked slowly to meet the Huns who were running towards them.

They were rapidly disarmed, and marched off under the command of an elderly man who afterwards turned out to be the equipment officer of the squadron, whilst another party vainly endeavoured to put out the flames of the burning machine. A few minutes later they were brought before the squadron commander, who addressed them in fair English, but, finding that he was likely to learn little from them, soon gave orders for their temporary confinement pending transfer to a more secure spot.

By now it was getting late in the evening, and from the room in which they were confined—for whether by accident or because two rooms were not available they were left together—they could see the German aeroplanes return for the night. Ten machines arrived, large reconnaissance two-seaters, similar to their own which had been destroyed, and one by one were housed in the hangars. Great consternation prevailed when the effect of the British bomb-raid was seen, and it became evident that two machines, the only ones which had not proceeded on the raid, had been destroyed before they could be taken from the hangars. Hence the immunity from attack of the British bombing squadron.

Whilst the two British officers sat wondering as to their ultimate destination, a German orderly appeared, presented the compliments of the Squadron Commander, and stated that the officers would be glad of their company for the evening meal. In great surprise, pilot and observer looked at each other and rose to accompany the man.

Somewhat unexpectedly the evening began well. The prisoners were not made to feel their position too keenly, and were treated almost as brother officers—certainly as guests. The squadron commander and several others understood English, whilst the pilot spoke German well, and conversation took a general turn, subjects apt to become controversial being mutually avoided. As the evening grew older, however, the hosts grew noisier and their gutturals deeper. At last one made a disparaging remark about the British air service which was cheered by the others, and things began to look less pleasant for the prisoners. The pilot, however, was buoyed up by a secret hope, and did his best to convey to his companion that he should drink little, and remain unmoved amidst the insults now freely bestowed upon them.

Noisier and noisier grew the Germans, until at last the squadron commander arose and left the mess. One by one the others retired or dropped asleep in their chairs, until few remained, but among them was the equipment officer, who had taken charge of them when they landed on the aerodrome, and who throughout the evening had watched them intently. This officer came over to the prisoners, and commenced speaking in a low voice. The others were too far gone in slumber or drink to pay any attention to his actions.

"Listen," he exclaimed. "My wife is English, and is in Eng-

39

land now. For months I have been unable to communicate with her. Take this message and I will arrange your escape."

Pilot and observer looked at each other. Was this true, or merely a plan to add to the pain of their captivity?

"Come," continued the German. "I will escort you to your room and explain on the way how you can effect your escape. In a few minutes I will arrange for a machine to be taken out of the hangar to have the engine tested. You will hear the roar of the engine from your room, and must arrange to get out— here is a key which will fit the lock—overcome your guard, and proceed to the machine when you hear the engine stop, for the mechanics will have been called away. Then you must take your chance of starting up again and getting off. And you will give this letter to my wife, and tell her of your escape, only do not mention how it was achieved—I wish to rejoin her after the war. Here is your room; the sentry does not understand English. Goodbye, good luck."

He turned and left them, and they heard the lock click as they stood speechless, gazing at each other. The pilot felt in his pocket and produced the letter; it was really true and not a dream.

They waited impatiently for the sound of the firing engine, hardly thinking it would be heard. At last the roar of the big Benz broke on the stillness of the night. Again they looked at each other, and the pilot removed the key from his pocket and silently slipped it in the lock. It turned noiselessly.

"Ready?" queried the pilot.

The observer nodded.

Back swung the door. The sentry was leaning against the wall, his rifle in the crook of his arm. Before he could grasp the situation his weapon was snatched away, and he lay senseless on the floor, stunned with the butt of his own rifle. Down the stairs silently sped the two airmen, and out into the night. As they reached the open the roaring engine slowed down, the noise ceased, and silence reigned. A voice called and was answered from the direction of the machine. Presently two forms were dimly seen moving away in the darkness, and pilot and observer walked boldly over the grass to the waiting aeroplane. The pilot climbed into the seat and fingered the controls. They were strange to him, but at last he felt the switch and throttle lever and called out to the waiting observer. That worthy slowly turned the air-screw until the correct stroke was reached, and with a violent pull set the blades swinging in the air. Quickly he rushed round the planes and clambered into his seat. Before he was settled down he felt the machine begin to move over the ground as the roar of the engine increased, and in a few seconds, which seemed hours, the aeroplane lifted into the air.

A moment later the "Tr-t-t-t" of a machine-gun opened up, but the airmen were speedily lost in the darkness, and in temporary safety.

Steering by compass, the pilot flew steadily towards home, and at last the twinkling lights of an aerodrome, laid out for the benefit of returning night raiders, showed him a spot on which to land.

Slowly the machine sank earthwards, and at last stopped close to the hangars.

"Hands up!" called a voice, and both pilot and observer meekly obeyed. Promptly they complied with the order to get out, and then explained the situation, and asked where they were. A slightly incredulous officer suggested that he had better verify their story before making them too comfortable, but as a short telephone conversation easily convinced him of the truth of their statements both officers were soon tucked away in bed, awaiting full morning before flying the prize back to their own aerodrome.

7

"Switch Off!"

A slight mist covered the morning sun as the two pilots strolled out on to the aerodrome; clouds were scattered intermittently over the sky, and a low haze betokened a hot day to come. The officers walked to their aeroplanes, which already awaited them outside the hangars, asked a few questions of the waiting mechanics, and returned to the sheds for coats and gloves. They then compared times, glanced at each other's maps to verify certain markings, and climbed into their respective machines.

A few minutes later the regular roar of an engine, followed soon after by the deep note of a second, proclaimed the beginning of a day's work, and the two scouts bounded over the surface of the aerodrome for a few yards, and then shot up into the air at an astonishing angle—an angle which seemed a momentary stunt, but which continued until both aeroplanes were tiny specks in the distance when seen from the aerodrome.

Very few minutes sufficed to take the pilots over the line and into enemy country. Until now both had been flying easily with no special vigilance, but the time had come when events might be expected at any moment, and it behoved the airmen to keep their eyes open for any hostile aircraft, as well as movements on the earth which might be turned to good account.

The right-hand pilot was the first to discern the distant specks which he immediately recognised as enemy aeroplanes. There were three of them at a slightly higher altitude than himself, and away to the north-east, and he recognised that a surprise attack from above would probably obtain at least one victim from among the three Huns. He therefore drew the other pilot's attention to the approaching trio, pushed up the nose of his machine, opened out the engine, and vanished into the clouds. It was his intention to await the approach of the enemy and then shoot down from above, surprising the Huns, and probably securing a victim before his presence was realised. Then with the help of his companion the other two could be easily dealt with.

Unfortunately Fate was against him, for when he dived through the clouds, expecting to see the Hun machines below, they were nowhere in the vicinity. As he looked around him a sudden flutter caused his eyes to travel to his map, but he was only in time to see it streaming away in the backwash of the propeller. It had been imperfectly secured, and the rush of the dive had blown it overboard. Further to complicate matters his companion was nowhere to be seen, so he determined to carry on alone, and steer by compass. He knew the ground below very well, having frequently flown over it, and carried an accurate picture of the map in his mind.

The mist had not vanished from the face of the sun, but the clouds were more broken, so the pilot determined to fly at a higher altitude, keeping hidden in the mist and flying west by his compass. This, he calculated, would carry him over a country which he knew, and by occasionally coming out of his hiding-place he could verify his position, and incidentally pick up any enemy aircraft which happened to be at hand.

So far so good. The rolling banks of damp vapour proved an effectual screen, and he remained hidden, flying steadily west until a break in the clouds showed him a glimpse of the ground below.

"Strange," he muttered; "don't seem to recognise the place."

While he puzzled his brains as to his locality, the mist swept around him again, and once more he had to trust to the compass.

After a few minutes, during which he watched the compass,

which swung idly from side to side, he decided that something was wrong, and dropped a thousand feet to locate himself. By this time he should have been in the vicinity of a large town, and his appearance from the clouds would have caused a tremendous shower of "Archies." Instead he gazed down upon a flat, open country. One or two little villages were dotted over the plain, but not a sign of any large town could be discerned on the horizon. Not one familiar landmark could he descry. He was hopelessly lost, and the best thing that he could do would be to get home as soon as possible. But in which direction did home lie? The only thing that he could do would be to fly into the face of the sun, keeping that luminary on his left.

This course would enable him to keep in one direction, and he could land near a village and inquire his whereabouts.

Shortly after making this decision he saw a town come up on the horizon, and he approached warily, flying low to avoid the clouds, and in momentary expectation of a shower of shells from the batteries below.

As his approach called forth no such hostile demonstration, he circled over the place, through which a river ran, and espying a large common close by, throttled down his engine to have a closer look A railway ran beside the river, and on this a large party of Germans were working, but as the pilot naturally concluded that the enemy could ill spare their own men for fatigues when prisoners in plenty were available, he took them for men captured by either the French or British, and this satisfied him that the common would be a good place on which to land.

He made a good landing, and, keeping his engine running, taxied over in the direction of a passing peasant. The pilot beckoned, and the man came up close to the machine in order to make himself heard above the noise of the running engine.

"Is this town occupied by French or British troops?" he queried in bad French.

The native stared at him in surprise, and then poured forth a voluble flow of words. From the torrent the pilot gathered that the town was neither held by French nor British, but by the

Boche. He had landed in a hornet's nest and had best escape whilst he could. Hurriedly he inquired in which direction lay the trenches, opened up his engine, and took off. As he flew over the town a tornado of artillery and machine-gun fire burst around him, but he reached the shelter of the clouds without damage, and carried on in the direction in which lay safety.

Suddenly in the mist two shapes loomed up, and the pilot just had time to recognise the black cross before he shot between them and vanished in the clouds. He turned and dived through the white vapour, seeking his foes, but they were not to be seen. The pilot decided to wait and see if they reappeared, but as he circled just below the clouds they dropped earthwards some distance away, and finally came to rest on an aerodrome close by a neighbouring town. As he was not positively anxious for a fight, the pilot left them and once more flew steadily in the direction of home.

Several times he descended to within a few hundred feet of the ground in order to locate himself, but each time the grey-green-clad figures which scattered at his approach showed him that the end of his journey was farther ahead yet.

Town after town was passed; he thought he recognised one or two, but as they were all so similar he dared not trust to appearances. On he flew through the mist, ever hoping to see some familiar landmark. Even if it were in the enemy's hands it would enable him to find himself, and take away the feeling of being so hopelessly lost.

At this time, too, a fresh terror arose—his petrol was giving out. Another few minutes, half an hour at the most, and he would be forced to land whatever his position. And as he looked at the gauge the engine spluttered. He started and almost gave himself up for lost, but, recollecting in time, he pumped furiously at the pressure, and the regular firing of his engine assured him that he was not finished yet.

Another gap in the clouds enabled him to see the ground, and he quickly picked out an aerodrome. He felt he must get a closer view of the place, come what might, and even as he decided the engine gave a final splutter and the propeller ceased to revolve.

Automatically he put down the nose of his machine and circled round the aerodrome. No aeroplanes were visible, and he had no means of telling whether he was landing in friendly or hostile country. Minute by minute he swept lower and lower; he was holding her up as long as possible. He longed for the ending of his suspense, but felt physically unable to stop the affair by landing quickly. At last the machine touched ground and ran to a standstill. He was unable to look out and see the men whom he knew must be coming out to him. He was incapable of doing more than lie back in his seat with his eyes closed, waiting to hear the first words. Would they be guttural command or a softer request?

Then the words came:

"Switch off, sir!"

8

With the Kite-Balloon Section

For some unknown reason the work of the Kite-Balloon Section of the Royal Air Force rarely receives the acknowledgments which are its due. The officer observers who ascend in baskets encounter a full share of the dangers of the air without the possibility of directly hitting back. True, through their work they hit back and hit hard in the best way—with heavy guns.

Before an officer of the K.-B.S. proceeds overseas he goes through a long course of free and captive ballooning, and of spotting for artillery. Perhaps he may be drafted to a unit working with the Navy, but more often he is sent over to co-operate with the gunners.

It is not generally known that the shape of the kite-balloons, sausages with bulging fins at the sides of one end and underneath, is due to the hunt for a stable position to observe from. The spherical captive balloon usually keeps up a rotatory motion, sickening the unfortunate observer, making it impossible for him to concentrate on his work. The shape of the envelope now in use ensures steadiness.

Slung from the gas-bag is a wicker basket containing telephones and other instruments, whilst attached to the sides on the exterior are several conical structures looking like candle snuffers. These are the parachutes to which the observers often have to trust their lives. Usually two officers are sent up together in the basket.

Observation is carried out at all hours of the day when visibility is good enough. The balloons ascend at the end of a cable some little distance behind the lines, and when sufficient altitude has been reached work commences.

Arrangements have probably been made previous to the ascent as to what positions are to be shelled, when a known object is in view, and the observer advises the battery when he is ready to commence. A single shot may be fired, the burst observed, and a correction sent to the battery. The next shot is closer, another correction is sent, and so on until the right range is found, all the battery being ranged on to the target until it is wiped out.

Then the observer trains the guns on to target number two, and the game continues.

A good observer will frequently at the same time train two or three batteries on to as many different targets with complete success.

Were this all, the life of those who occupy the basket would be simple; but it must not be imagined that the Huns allow the K.-B.S. to work unmolested. In many cases the work of observation is interrupted by a German machine told off to drive down the balloon. If this aeroplane can avoid the protecting patrol which usually guards the balloons, the chances are that the observers' lives will be filled with excitement.

Out of the clouds suddenly dives a scout, flying straight at the balloon. Anti-aircraft fire opens on the raider, and the sky is dotted with puffs of smoke. These the Hun, nose down, all out, has no difficulty in avoiding, and when within range pours out a stream of incendiary bullets. He can scarcely miss so large a target.

Those below commence to haul down the balloon, hoping to bring it to safety before much damage is done. The observers, if unhit amidst the storm of bullets, have the choice of remaining where they are, taking the chance of being hauled down safely, or jumping overboard, trusting to the parachute.

If the latter choice is made, they climb over the edge of the basket and drop into space. The parachutes are always attached firmly to their bodies, and the fall pulls them from their cases.

For a moment the men whistle through the air; then the fabric opens, steadies the descent, and they slowly drift with the wind towards earth.

This is the moment sometimes chosen by German pilots for an absolutely unnecessary cruelty. Having destroyed the balloon, or at least forced it to descend, the pilot turns his guns on the helplessly drifting observers, using them as the target on which to practise shooting; but often he is driven off before he can achieve his object, and the observers' fall continues.

If they jump overboard at a great height and the wind blows in the direction of the German lines they may descend only to be captured on arrival. Should better luck attend them, they fall in the British lines, alighting with only the force of about a six-foot drop.

9

Humour of the Air

Whilst humour has almost vanished from terrestrial warfare, it still occupies a prominent place in the life of the air. Not only do pilots behave like the schoolboys they in many cases are, whilst behind the lines, but frequently jests are carried out far over the enemy's country. Often the jest takes a grim turn, as in the following affair.

On a certain part of the line one British squadron had established such a reputation among the enemy that few German machines waited for our aeroplanes to approach within range of machine-gun fire. The sight of red, white and blue rings caused the Huns to hurry back to their aerodromes with all speed. Although their landing grounds were bombed nightly and single British machines hung about inviting combat, no German could be found to accept the challenge.

Blowing holes in aerodromes soon tired our pilots, and a scheme was devised by means of which it was hoped to liven up the enemy a little.

Early one morning, before the mist had properly dispersed, the squadron commander crossed the lines, carrying an ordinary brown paper parcel. He sought out the largest aerodrome, and, flying low, fired a few shots into the hangars to attract attention. As usual, no reply was made to his fire, neither did any aeroplane attempt to put off to attack him.

He then descended quite close to the ground, and dropped his parcel just outside the hangars. Having done this, he put

50

up the nose of his machine and vanished in the mist to await events.

First one, then another, German crept out to examine the parcel. None dared touch it; for all they knew, it was a disguised bomb which would explode directly the string was untied. Quite a crowd collected. Finally an expert arrived, the crowd hurriedly dispersed, and an effort was made to explode the "bomb."

After several efforts which had no effect, a rifle was produced, and several shots fired into the parcel from a safe range. As no explosion resulted, the expert took his courage in both hands and gingerly undid the brown paper, exposing to view a pair of ordinary infantry boots with the following message attached:

If you won't come up here and fight, herewith one pair of boots for work on the ground. Pilots—for the use of.

Gradually the crowd reassembled to study the point of the joke, and marvel at the ways of the English.

This was the pilot's opportunity. Suddenly diving out of the hanging mist, he dropped two bombs on the party. The crowd dispersed, leaving the ground strewn with casualties, and the pilot, having fired a number of rounds into the buildings where the men had vanished, left for home.

This incident is akin to an effort in the early days of the war, when a pilot scattered a large body of troops forming up for attack by dropping a football in their midst. As the ball swayed to earth the Germans bolted in all directions, and even when their fears were allayed by the bouncing "bomb" the confusion which had been caused precluded all possibility of that particular attack being made.

An incident which shows that all Huns are not devoid of humour happened during the British advance on the Somme during 1916. A German aerodrome had to be hastily evacuated, so hastily that even the day's correspondence was left untouched in the German adjutant's office. On looking through the letters, one of the newly arrived British officers came across a bundle of much-minuted correspondence bearing on the question of repairs to a bridge over a brook which bounded the aerodrome. Evidently the German engineers had been unwilling to undertake the repairs, the Air Service too busy to spare the men, and the infantry otherwise employed. The correspondence had been passed from one to the other, gradually growing in bulk, finally returning to the aerodrome with the matter still undecided.

The German adjutant's last effort before retiring from the advancing British was to scribble hastily—

Min. 35.—To the British officer in command. Passed to you as this bridge is now in your hands.

The gentleman who suggested, on the amalgamation of the R.F.C. and R.N.A.S., that the R.F.C. carrier pigeons should amalgamate with parrots, so that their offspring might deliver messages verbally, was not thought worthy of any high decoration.

10

The End of the Day

As the evening drew on the C.O. and his remaining flight commander walked out on to the aerodrome to watch the return of the flock. Almost every machine in the squadron had gone out with a large formation nearly three hours before, and great things were expected of them. So far they had been extraordinarily lucky, and not a single aeroplane had been lost.

"Yes," remarked the flight commander, "if only the War Baby had led hearts we should have pulled through and won the rubber, but he was miles away up in the clouds thinking of that girl he met when he was on leave."

The squadron commander nodded.

"Talking of girls," went on his junior, "have you seen the three damsels of Ferféy? They keep an *estaminet* and lick the girls in the boot shop into a cocked hat."

Apparently the C.O. had been to Ferféy, for he chuckled sagely, and went on slashing at the thistles, which were rather plentiful just there. Ever and anon he glanced up in the direction from which the returning aeroplanes should appear.

They both remained silent for awhile, apparently lost in thought over the fair damsels of Ferféy.

Presently the Major broke the stillness.

"It's Friday, isn't it?" he queried.

"Yes, and the thirteenth."

No more was said, but each was conscious that the other was thinking that the machines were getting overdue.

"I told the sergeant-major to have that hole filled in," irritably remarked the C.O., pointing to a spot where a recent bomb from a raiding Hun had caused landing to become unpleasant.

"Go and tell him, there's a good fellow," he continued.

The flight commander walked off to do his bidding, while his senior remained nervously switching the thistles. He whistled softly to himself, trying to distract his thoughts and appear nonchalantly at ease.

"Friday and the thirteenth," he muttered presently.

The sun had now sunk so low that its rim was already dipping below the horizon. A red glow suffused the whole of the western sky, and the sun itself lay like a blood-red stain amidst its setting of fleecy clouds. But it was towards the east that the waiting officer so frequently turned his eyes. It is doubtful if he even noticed the ever-changing panorama of kaleidoscopic colour that covered the heavens. A small black speck against the darkening blueness would mean far more to him.

At last his face lit up, and he gazed unaffectedly into the east. A series of minute dots approached rapidly closer, and his practised eye at once recognised his own machines.

"Good formation," remarked the Flight Commander, who had returned unobserved.

His CO. disregarded the remark. He was counting the returning aeroplanes. They were two short.

At last the first machine touched ground and gently taxied up to the sheds.

The two officers walked over to it, noticing its shot-about appearance. Two coloured streamers proclaimed it to be the property of the formation leader, and that worthy soon jumped out and commenced looking over his machine.

"Pretty hot time?" asked the flight commander.

"Yes, pretty bad. Met the circus about ten miles over the other side, and poor young O'Brien and Cassidy seem to have been for it. Saw Cassidy go down in a spin, and O'Brien just dropped out of sight whilst I was busy with two Huns. One of them did this," he observed, pointing to the hole-spotted planes.

"'Archie' did that bit just as we were coming home," he continued, fingering a broken rib.

The C.O. nodded absently; his thoughts were with O'Brien and Cassidy.

One by one the machines landed and disgorged their passengers, who stood about in twos and threes instead of wandering off to report on the day's work. Waiting mechanics pushed the aeroplanes into the hangars, and the night drew on.

Each group chatted quietly and individual officers glanced casually towards the east. There was still a possibility of the missing people arriving. A slim chance, perhaps, for all the others had been in for a good half-hour, but hope dies hard.

Suddenly a rocket fizzed up into the air, and burst, scattering its glowing lights into the night. A moment later another followed, its radiance causing strange shadows to be cast on the ground.

The waiting groups began to melt away. Night had come on; a hard day's work was finished, and there was, perhaps, a harder one to come.

Only the C.O. and the flight commander remained silently on the aerodrome. Each was thinking the same thought—thoughts of the boys who were gone; perhaps their turns would come soon; life in the air was uncertain; a sudden dive, a stream of lead, and all would be over. But Cassidy was married, married only a few months before to a girl from his own fresh green isle.

"Poor kid!" murmured the major, voicing their common thought.

And then in the silence of the night came the sound of an engine. Another rocket shot up and a minute later the aeroplane rumbled up to the sheds.

"Who is it?" demanded the C.O.

"Faith, an' it's both of us. Major dear," replied a rich young brogue. "An' did ye give us up for lost at all? But ye needn't have. I got rather badly shot about, and spun down, and was forced to land, but luckily no one worried about me, and presently O'Brien here just dropped down and picked me up. That's all, and a good day it's been." He laughed at the recollection.

And then the major's feelings gave way.

"What the blazes do you mean standing there laughing like a young fool? Get your machine in and send in your report at once."

He stopped abruptly, and, linking his arm in that of the flight commander, walked off towards the mess.

11

Pistols for Two—
(a duel of the air)

To see three enemy machines all falling over one another in their haste to escape from a solitary British scout, gives a feeling of great satisfaction to the pilot concerned.

When this occurred in the neighbourhood of a certain large enemy aerodrome, the pilot began to think. He had sighted three Albatross scouts, each aeroplane a fair match for his own machine. Naturally he attacked, diving at them, but before he was within range they put down their noses and ran.

At five hundred feet one of them side-slipped and crashed on the aerodrome, the second reached ground and crashed in its haste to escape, turning completely over, whilst the third landed safely, the pilot hurriedly leaving his machine, and running for shelter.

The British pilot, rather amused at the practical illustration of the saying "More haste less speed," planed slowly down in circles, intending to use his machine-gun on the hangars, generally to annoy the people on the aerodrome and possibly do a certain amount of damage. Should any aeroplane try to put off to attack, he was confident of his ability to shoot it down before it had much more than left the ground.

Unfortunately his design was frustrated by the arrival of another German scout of a different type, which dived at him, compelling him to swing round and face his opponent.

Then followed a duel of aerobatics as each pilot manoeu-vred for the position from which he could best deal with his foe. Each machine was fast and handy; both pilots were experi-enced, old hands at the game—the duel of life and death. Burst after burst was exchanged as one or other machine came for an instant in the arc of its opponent's fire. Time after time flames burst from the muzzles of the guns, and pauses ensued whilst the pilots changed their drums of ammunition.

Zooming, banking, spiralling, side-slipping, looping—all the arts of the air were tried, and neither had the advantage. At last the ammunition of the British pilot gave out, and all his wits were taxed to avoid his enemy.

But he was not finished, though his last cartridge had been used. As a last resort he took his Colt automatic pistol in hand and charged at the Hun.

Astonished at this move, and expecting to be run down, the German lost his head for an instant—long enough for the Brit-ish pilot to close with his enemy and discharge his pistol from the range of a few yards.

The German scout wavered and stalled, side-slipped and spun, finally breaking in the air, the pieces falling to join the wrecked machines on the aerodrome below.

12

Over the Rhine

As the first grey light of morning broke through the darkness, six big bombers were brought from their hangars and lined up on the aerodrome. Trolleys soon appeared laden with huge pear-shaped bombs and busy mechanics quickly adjusted them on the bomb ribs attached to the underside of the planes. Bowden wires were tested to see that all the dropping apparatus was in order, then the tanks of the aeroplanes were filled with petrol and oil, belts of ammunition placed in position by the guns, and at last, after a final inspection, the machines were pronounced in order, the mechanics standing by to await the arrival of the officers.

Most of the pilots had arrived early, personally superintending the fitting of their aeroplanes, and running up their engines. The observers came later, only worrying about guns, maps and supply of ammunition.

When all preparations were completed, some tiny scouts were wheeled out, looking like mosquitoes beside their giant brethren.

These soon left the ground, and climbed up into the growing light. They were the protecting escort to the slower and more cumbersome bombers.

One by one the huge aeroplanes left the ground, climbing in circles to the altitude where the scouts were already awaiting them. A few manoeuvres, and then, at a signal from the leader, all machines fell into formation and headed east into the growing day.

No notice was taken of their passage over the trenches; probably the German gunners could not see them owing to their altitude and the thin mist which covered the ground at that early hour of the morning.

Steadily east flew the formation, the bombers forming a triangle with the leader at the apex, whilst the scouts flew ahead, behind, and above the formation, with others at either side about the same height. Occasionally a machine would do an S turn to lose distance as it gained somewhat on its companions, but generally the formation was excellent, and the aeroplanes, some fifteen thousand feet in the air, swept steadily towards their objective.

At last a thin ribbon of silver was visible ahead; the objective, a famous Rhine town, was at hand. Some distance away to the right could be seen the puffs of bursting shells, and amidst them the glint of sunlight on aeroplanes. Evidently another formation which was bombing a different place was hard at work. The leader smiled grimly when he thought the town ahead would be well prepared for their visit. He was used to "Archie," and realised what a bad shelling meant.

A moment later the storm burst. Puffs of cotton-wool-like smoke dotted the sky above, below, and on all sides of the machines, but no damage was done. Then the formation leader gave the signal to separate, and the bombers scattered, each pilot preparing to drop his bombs where he thought they might be most effective.

One after another the aeroplanes deposited their loads, the scouts meanwhile fighting off the cloud of German fighters which had ascended to destroy the raiders. Shells no longer burst in the air; friends were as likely to suffer as foes. Instead the air echoed with the "Rat-tat-tat-tat" of guns fitted with interrupter gears, while every few seconds the dull boom of a bomb exploding far below added to the turmoil.

One by one the "eggs" were laid, and the bombers drew off. The leader was the last to try his luck, as he wished to observe

clearly the effect of the explosions. Two roaring fires and a thick
pall of black smoke indicated much damage to what were believed to be factories, and in the bright light of the now fully-
risen sun he discerned damage to the railway station, where a
big hole gaped in the roof, and to the track outside the station.
So far the great bridge over the Rhine seemed undamaged, so
he dipped his machine, and, amidst a tornado of fire descended
to within a few hundred feet, dropping two heavy bombs almost
simultaneously, severing the railway over the river, and tearing a
huge gap in the heavy masonry of the bridge.

His work accomplished, he opened up the throttle and
climbed into the sky. Had his engine failed he would most certainly have met with death in the descent, but his luck held, and
he quickly rose many thousands of feet towards his comrades,
who were hastening away now that the work of destruction was
complete.

Unfortunately his solitary state attracted three of the German
machines, which attacked from different quarters. Both he and
his observer fought gallantly, but had not one of the scouts noticed what was happening and dived to his rescue, the machine
would undoubtedly have been lost. As it was, one Hun plane
crashed to earth in flames, stricken by the bullets poured from
the scout machine, and another left the combat evidently badly
damaged. The third fled.

Once clear of the town the leader signalled for his bombers
to reform for better protection, and with the scouts fighting a
rear-guard action, the sun and wind at their backs, they sped
westwards.

One by one the German machines left the attack as they got
farther from their base, until the scouts were in their old positions on the lookout for danger, from above.

"Archie" greeted them as they crossed the trenches. At last
the aerodrome was sighted, the signal to disperse was given, and
each plane descended, the officers conscious of having done a
good morning's work and ready to do justice to the breakfast
which awaited them.

13

An Airman's Christmas

Christmas Eve and the prospect of a quiet day to follow. The pilot, sitting alone in the mess, felt at peace with the world, warm and contented with his lot. He had been out early in the morning on an offensive patrol, and again in the evening. Though he had not encountered a Hun on mischief bent, and had only endured the usual small strafe from "Archie," the very fact of being ten thousand feet in the air with the thermometer showing 10 degrees of frost at ground level and goodness only knows how many at that altitude was sufficient to make the best-tempered pilot somewhat peevish, and he was now undergoing the consequent reaction and felt at peace with all the world.

The mess, some fifteen miles behind the lines, was sufficiently safe to ensure repose—the only possibility of disturbance being from some marauding Hun—and the warmth and quiet of the place contrasted pleasantly with the noise and racket which he had just left.

Except for himself the mess was empty. Some few of the other officers were employed with their machines or in their quarters, but the large majority were out on a bomb raid some thirty miles the other side of the lines. Next day everyone expected a rest, for so far the only orders received from the Wing were for the usual morning patrols.

The door opened, admitting a blast of air and two half-frozen pilots. The raiders were returning well pleased with their work, having bombed a dump and an important railway junction. Each pilot was sure that his bombs had hit the mark, and some of the observers outran the pilots in their certainty.

The warmth, feeling of success and knowledge of a slack day to follow put everyone in a good temper. Even the unfortunate individuals selected for the following day's patrols succumbed to the feeling of good fellowship; probably the feel of Christmas in the air had something to do with it. Everyone was talking at once, the gramophone blared out the latest record, just received in a Christmas hamper, people eagerly opened parcels and exhibited queer presents from anxious aunts, boxes of Fortnum and Mason's provisions, the latest copies of the *Sketch* and *Tatler*, and all the seasonable magazines—in fact, all the appurtenances of Christmas at the front; pandemonium, the happy pandemonium of youth, reigned supreme.

The evening passed as other evenings, or almost as other evenings, in cards and a certain amount of ragging. One by one the various officers walked off to bed, until only the Squadron Commander and one or two others were left. As they prepared to move also, an orderly thrust his head in at the door with a request that the recording officer would speak on the telephone—he was wanted by the Wing. The C.O. and a flight commander exchanged glances; both had a premonition of what would happen. In a few minutes the R.O. returned, his face explaining to those present as well as any words the news he had to impart.

"Bomb raid on aerodrome at D—— at dawn, as reprisal for one they have just executed on one of ours," he jerked out. The C.O. cursed under his breath, and walked over to his office to arrange details of bombs, formation, and method of attack. Those left in the mess seated themselves to await orders before proceeding to bed. These were soon received, and a few minutes later the place was in darkness.

Four-thirty a.m. on December 25th is not exactly a cheery time, nor is a bomb raid an ideal way of spending Christmas. At that time the sheds were already showing signs of activity, minor repairs and alterations were being carried out on machines, bullet holes being patched in planes, and the tanks being filled with oil and petrol. One by one the aeroplanes were wheeled out into the darkness of before the dawn, their planes showing greyly in the blackness, until they were lined up, twelve in all, their ribs loaded with bombs, and Lewis guns peering venomously over the nacelles.

About five o'clock the first officer arrived on the scene, climbed into his seat, tested the controls, and gave the signal to the waiting mechanic:

"Contact."

The roar of the engine broke the stillness as it gradually gathered in volume, and at last died away. One by one other engines took up the note, until the air vibrated with noise. A few last instructions, and the pilots went to their machines, made certain of a few points with the observers, and one by one left the ground, and up into the sky.

By this time the blackness of night was getting less dense, but the cold of the frosty air bit deep into the flyers' bones.

The pilot of the night before who had been promising himself an easy day was stationed at the tail of one side of the V formation chosen for the raid. As he circled round gaining height and awaiting the signal to set off he caught himself thinking of the last Christmas spent at home. This one would be very different, but he was thoroughly determined to make the Huns, who were responsible for spoiling his day, have a most unsatisfactory time themselves.

Below him he could dimly discern the outline of the country, the fields and roads passed over, and faintly in front he could just make out the shape of the machine before him. At last he saw the outline of the trenches, dim gashes in the surrounding land, and prepared himself for the strafe which would shortly commence, for it was gradually growing lighter and "Archie" would not miss the chance of so good a target. He was last in the line, and so likely to get a good share of it. Also he would probably be the attempted prey of any marauding Hun who chose to make a dive out of the clouds in the hope of securing a victim before breakfast. Altogether he had to keep his eyes open.

The strafe soon commenced, and the air was dotted with balls of smoke. Whether it was because the light was poor or because the German gunners were sleepy he could not tell, but the shooting was bad, and the bursts all below him. It soon ceased and the formation continued steadily towards its objective.

The pilot's attention was attracted soon after this by a signal from the leader of the formation, showing that they had nearly reached their destination, and should prepare to attack. Another signal showed somewhere ahead, and the observer looked round to the pilot with anticipation in his eyes.

One by one the machines ahead throttled down their engines, and shot earthwards through the dawn. At the prearranged height each aeroplane dropped its complement of bombs, and blazes of light showed that some of them had proved effective. At last his turn came. He pulled back the throttle lever and dipped the nose of his machine. The air whistled through the wires and struts. Carefully looking through the sight he pulled the release six times, and six bombs dropped to the ground below. In the growing light he saw one take effect on a hangar, and chuckled as he thought that Christmas was not wasted after all.

Throughout this attack the enemy had not remained quiet, and the air was filled with clouds of smoke from bursting shells. So thickly was the air plastered with bursts that it was impossible to manoeuvre to avoid them, and the pilot turned quickly to resume his place in the formation and return to his aerodrome. Also several German machines had been brought out from the hangars, and were preparing to ascend. Work finished, home was decidedly the best place.

Formation was quickly resumed, and amidst a perfect tornado of anti-aircraft fire the aeroplanes set their noses towards home.

One by one they landed safely on the aerodrome. As the last machine pulled up and the sounds of the engines died away, the bells of a neighbouring church could be heard ringing for Mass.

The C.O. looked at his watch with a smile on his face; it was just after eight.

"Now for Christmas," he remarked to himself as he walked off to the mess.

14

Night Observation

Spending a few hours aloft in a free balloon during the dark hours of a wintry night is not a pleasant method of passing one's time, but is part of the daily work of a certain section of the Royal Air Force.

Large towns which have suffered in the past by bombs dropped from Zeppelins and Gothas have learnt the wisdom of shielding their lights and making their factories inconspicuous.

It is for the purpose of detecting any signs which may show the vulnerable points of these towns that the balloon ascents are made.

One afternoon when a slight wind blows steadily from the right direction, the aeronaut has the envelope filled with gas, and when darkness has set in climbs into the basket, well muffled in warm clothes, for here is no engine to warm him, sees that his electric torch, thermos flask, maps and notebook are ready, then gives the signal for the ascent.

Slowly the balloon climbs until well clear of any surrounding obstructions, then the rope connecting it with the ground party below is released, and the gas-bag shoots rapidly upwards.

A very few minutes suffice to carry the pilot to the required altitude, which he maintains, increases, or decreases as circumstances necessitate by means of valves and ballast. The former are opened to permit the escape of gas when it is desired to reach a lower altitude, while ballast is discharged if the balloon is required to ascend. Generally the same height is maintained throughout the flight.

Having attained the correct position, the pilot proceeds to look around him. A gentle wind is steadily sweeping him across the sleeping city, and far below he can dimly discern its darkened streets and squares. Pin-points of light here and there show that some householders have not shaded their windows sufficiently, but nothing appears which calls for special comment.

Suddenly a beam of light shines across the sky, wavering, hither and thither, seeking possible prey. It is the beam of a searchlight, manoeuvred by the men who are ready at a moment's notice to concentrate their lights on any hostile aircraft which may appear, in order that the anti-aircraft batteries may throw up a barrage of protective shells.

A moment later the pencil light falls across the balloon, making everything in the wicker basket as clear as daylight. A signal flashes out, is answered by the pilot, then the beam withdraws and recommences stabbing the darkness of the sky. Should the pilot fail to give the answering signal correctly every battery in the place would be trained on him and the balloon rapidly shot down.

For a few minutes after the searchlight withdraws the pilot is unable to see into the dense darkness, but gradually his night-sight returns, and he recommences his search.

A blaze of red light draws his attention to a particular spot, and he carefully notes the position on his map for report next day. Evidently a factory is working at full blast, but means must be devised to hide the telltale light.

The pilot looks at his watch. Already he has been in the air for over an hour.

The night is cold, making him shiver as he unscrews the thermos flask and proceeds to take his supper. He is interrupted once by signals from the ground, and then the moon begins to rise.

Clearer and clearer grow the outlines of houses and streets; railways, stations, canals, and parks are sharply defined in the silver light. Ponds glow like burnished silver. Every detail of the city is thrown up in relief except those parts where the smoke of the ever-working factories casts a black pall over the buildings, camouflaging the very parts the Hun most wishes to damage.

In the clear light the pilot proceeds to find, with the aid of his map, the position of all protecting anti-aircraft batteries. Though he knows the exact spots where they should be seen, he is unable to discover any signs of their presence, and notes that their camouflage is perfect.

Slowly the balloon drifts until the out-skirts of the city are reached, when the pilot decides to descend. As the country becomes clear of buildings he opens the valve, falling gradually as the gas escapes.

He has arranged previously for a party to await him at a certain spot and soon he lets down a rope, which is seized from below, the balloon being rapidly hauled down.

Gathering up his goods, the pilot enters the waiting car, leaving his men to deflate the gas-bag, and returns to the city and bed.

15

The Outsider's Race

"Archie" makes the long reconnaissance a thing not to be undertaken lightly, and though this particular job is disliked more on account of its monotony than its danger, occasionally incidents occur which make the pilot realise that his job is not altogether destitute of excitement.

Two officers were detailed for this particular piece of work, and received orders to reconnoitre a stretch of country well in the heart of Belgium.

All went right and without incident until the outward journey was nearly completed, when the pilot noticed that his engine was not running well and that the revolutions were dropping. He therefore decided to return by the shortest route, taking photographs of two important points during the journey. This decision he communicated to the observer, who, realising that nothing else could be done, agreed to this course.

Luckily they were flying at a great height, for when but a short way on the homeward journey the engine spluttered and finally cut out. Nothing daunted, the pilot pushed down the nose of his aeroplane, realising that with his great altitude and a following wind he had a good chance of gliding over the lines before landing.

Just then the observer leaned over and tapped him on the shoulder, drawing his attention to a number of specks in the rear. He was not sure what these specks were, but as he could not alter his tactics whether the approaching specks were friends or foes, he held on his course. In due course the aeroplane was over-taken sufficiently for the observer to make out that the specks were ten in number, and a little later he was able to distinguish the black cross painted on the planes.

Pilot and observer looked one another in the face. Death seemed certain. Even if the engine had been running and the pilot able to manoeuvre so that their guns could be used to advantage, the odds of ten to one—ten scouts to one comparatively slow reconnaissance machine—were too great to contemplate with any hope of success.

Little by little the Huns approached, until the leading scout came within range and poured out a stream of bullets. In his excitement the Hun shot wildly, and his bullets went wide of the mark. A moment later the first burst from the British machine caught the scout fair in the middle of the fuselage; a sheet of flame shot up, the pilot was seen to fall forward in his seat, and the aeroplane plunged earthwards, a blazing mass.

Nine scouts were left, and the British machine was unable to attack its aggressors. Three Huns dived at the unfortunate aeroplane, jets of flame spurting from their machine-guns. One of these received the second burst from the observer's gun, a plane collapsed and the scout spun slowly down, crashing many thousands of feet below.

To avoid the fire of the other Germans the pilot swung his machine round and brought the forward gun into action. This drove off one of the aggressors, and enabled the observer to keep the others at such a distance that their fire was uncertain and vague. They had learned to respect the accurate shooting of the British officers, and for some time none of the scouts ventured within range, the whole pack hanging about like jackals chasing a wounded lion.

Time was now the prime factor of safety for the British machine. Provided the observer could keep the foe at bay long enough, the pilot felt certain of being able to cross the lines before being forced to land. He still had about eight thousand feet height left, and would be able to glide for a considerable distance. The wind was freshening and things looked hopeful.

Then the Huns decided to attack again, and flew at the solitary machine from all quarters. Bursts of fire were directed at first one, then another of the attackers, and for a time the observer kept them all at bay. The planes were pierced with bullet holes in many places, one broken rib peered through the torn fabric, but the controls remained intact, and so far both of the officers were unhurt.

At last a shot hit the observer, wounding him in the arm, but he managed to stick to his gun and fire fresh bursts at the Huns. In the short pauses which ensued between the savage dives of their aggressors he bandaged up the wound and stopped the flow of blood. Another shot grazed his forehead, but with blood streaming down his face he carried on. Then the pilot was hit, his leg being broken, hindering his control of the machine. As there was little to do except continue the straight glide he was able to carry on, bandaging up the leg as the machine flew ahead.

Glancing at his aneroid, the pilot noticed that there was barely a couple of thousand feet left. Looking before him he saw the line of the trenches. Then "Archie" burst out in all his severity; the air became clouded with bursts; shrapnel whistled through the air; one jagged fragment of shell tore a gaping hole in the plane, narrowly missing the main spar. But all the time the trenches and safety crept closer and closer.

Probably because of the low altitude "Archie" was unable to bring down the damaged machine, and only succeeded in keeping off the Hun scouts, which did not venture near in case they should receive one of the bursts meant for the British machine. As "Archie" realised that he was becoming ineffective the machine-guns and rifles in the trenches took up the tale, and a hot fire was concentrated on the aeroplane as it glided over the lines barely two hundred feet from the ground.

As the pilot saw the outline of the trenches pass beneath him he felt his senses fading away. He was awakened to consciousness by the observer, who leaned over and aroused him from his stupor. In a vague way he held up the nose of the machine as it carried on over No Man's Land. The British trenches were still some hundred yards away, and his momentary lapse had allowed the machine to lose a little of their precious height. Again he felt himself fading away into oblivion, but aroused himself with an effort, seeing the blood-stained face of the observer leaning anxiously over him.

A roar of cheering told him that the trenches were crossed. The ground was close beneath him, pitted with shell-holes scarred with trenches. Automatically he flattened out. Then came a crash, the machine pitched forward, and he lost consciousness.

When he came to he found that his observer had dragged him out of the machine which was lying crumpled up at the bottom of a shell-hole. It was useless to attempt to move as their position was well sheltered, and in order to do so they would have to expose themselves to the enemy's fire.

Unfortunately the Huns had observed the spot where the machine had crashed, and soon shells began to drop over in its vicinity. Had the pilot been able to move they would have made a rush for safety, but progress with his broken leg was bound to be slow. There seemed nothing to do except to lie close in the hole and hope for the best.

And the best happened. A field ambulance unit had noticed the crash, and during a pause in the shelling two men crept into the shell-hole, hastily improvised a means of carrying the wounded man, and then dashed for safety, the observer with them.

In a nearby communication trench they paused. Next moment a direct hit was obtained on the machine. Luckily the pilot had again fainted, and so did not witness the destruction of his beloved old bus.

16

A Miracle in the Air

One of the chief qualities required by a scout pilot is "dash." All our airmen are fearless, and many are first-class pilots, but the man in a scout machine must always be spoiling for a fight, careless of what odds he encounters, and full of reckless confidence in his own ability to beat six Huns.

A pilot with these necessary qualifications one day encountered a strong returning German patrol. Without hesitation he dashed at an aeroplane which lagged rather behind the others, though at a higher altitude. The German saw him coming, put down the nose of his machine, and tried to seek shelter with the patrol. He was, however, too late. The scout dived at its retreating prey, and when at close range the pilot fired a burst from his gun, sending the hostile machine spinning to earth, where it was smashed to pieces.

Meanwhile the remaining German machines had not been idle, for six had left the main body, and were making for the British scout.

Nothing daunted, the pilot charged into the formation, firing indiscriminately at any aeroplane which crossed his sights, diving, turning, twisting in and out among his foes. It was useless to attempt to concentrate his fire on any one machine for the other five would then be able to attack unmolested. Luckily, the scout was faster and handier by far than any of the German machines, so the pilot was for a time able to remain unharmed amidst the mixup.

Unfortunately his luck could not hold good for ever. At last a lucky shot hit the control lever, and the scout plunged helplessly earthwards, the pilot powerless to check the nose-dive through the air, and unable to reply to the storm of bullets which swept after him from the machines which followed him earthwards.

There was nothing to do but sit and wait for the crash. He wondered if he would feel it, and if death would be painful. In a vague way he thought of his past years, the school he had so recently left, the short period at Sandhurst, his training as a pilot.

He thought of the journey overseas with his squadron, his first fight in which he had sent his enemy spinning to his doom. Would he meet that pilot afterwards, he wondered. If so, would he be a friend or foe? Did the war continue after death? He was sick of the whole show, and glad to be out of it.

And still the machine plunged on, the wires screaming in the wind, the propeller revolving on account of the air pressure— the engine he had long since switched off.

It could be only a few seconds now; earth was very near.

By force of habit he unfastened the belt securing him in his seat.

Then the miracle happened. For no apparent reason the machine suddenly flattened out. So abruptly did it leave the vertical for the horizontal that the longerons of the fuselage snapped immediately beneath the pilot's seat. When this occurred the aeroplane was close to the ground, and long before she could again get into a vertical nosedive the crash came.

Considering all things it was a very little crash, and when the pilot recovered from a momentary stunning he discovered that he had been thrown clear of the wreckage, shaken, but otherwise unharmed.

Glancing upwards he saw his late adversaries circling above him, like carrion-crows waiting for their prey. Evidently his movement was seen, for a machine swooped at him, and when within about thirty feet of the ground opened fire from its gun. Another followed, and in succession each German fired at the British pilot. That worthy, not to be outdone, drew his revolver, returning the fire as each aeroplane came within range.

How long the unequal duel could have lasted it is impossible to say, but the arrival of three British scouts put a different complexion on matters. The pilot had a perfect view of the whole fight, which was carried on at a height of little more than a thousand feet. It did not occur to him that he was in some danger from the flying bullets. He merely stood cheering, entranced with excitement. Luckily for him no enemy troops were in the neighbourhood, or his pleasure might have been of short duration.

The three scouts made short work of their adversaries. Two of the Huns fell almost together, one in flames, the other with planes collapsed, spinning to earth. The remaining four fled, followed by two of the scouts, who relentlessly pursued them until they took refuge by landing, when one collided with a tree, whilst another turned over on its back, burying the pilot in the wreckage.

The remaining scout planed slowly down, and, as there was ample room, landed beside the man who had lived through such a miraculous escape. The latter ran up to the machine, the pilot meanwhile keeping his propeller slowly revolving. After the exchange of a few hurried remarks shouted above the noise of the engine, the stranded officer climbed up behind the pilot's seat, sitting on the edge of the cockpit, his legs dangling on either side of the pilot, holding on tightly to the struts of the machine.

When he was safely settled the scout bounded over the ground up into the air, making little of its double burden.

Once a German machine was sighted, but was avoided; a combat was not to be desired with the machine so awkwardly loaded; rather, both pilot and passenger desired to reach home without further excitements.

"Archie" opened on them as they crossed the trenches somewhat lower than usual, but no damage was done, and soon a long glide culminated in the safe landing of the aeroplane with its passenger, who had gone through as exciting a day as could well be expected even in the Royal Air Force.

17

Guns and Pyjamas

Complaints having been received that enemy, guns were particularly troublesome in a certain area, and that owing to the heavy ground-mist the kite-balloon observers had been unable to locate them, a machine was sent up to find their positions and direct the fire of British guns on to the emplacements.

Neither pilot nor observer had any particular liking for the job, for it meant a long search far over the lines, with an excellent chance of losing one's way in the mist, and being forced to land among the Huns. However, the job had to be done, so both officers put on an extra sweater, took care to fill their thermos flasks, and placed pyjamas, tooth-brush, and shaving tackle in a small case in the machine. It is as well to be prepared for eventualities, and obviate when possible some of the minor discomforts of a stay in Germany.

The aerodrome was soon lost in the mist which spread over the ground like a wet blanket, as the aeroplane headed for the lines without the preliminary circling for height which is usually carried out. The machine was a reconnaissance two-seater fitted with guns for pilot and observer, carrying a few small bombs tucked away under the wing-tips. Tempting targets some-times present themselves unexpectedly, so that it is as well not to neglect opportunities.

Over the trenches, which the pilot crossed at a very low altitude, the first signs of life were observed, and a terrific fusillade of machine-gun fire was opened on the aero-plane. "Archie," either because he could not see the target, or because he was unable to depress himself sufficiently, remained silent.

Comparative quiet soon reigned once the trenches were left behind, and the observer began to apply himself to the business of the day. The mist having cleared a little, he judged that they must be near the spot where the troublesome guns were supposed to lie. He peered down through the vapour, signalling the pilot to circle the machine over the district until he had examined it thoroughly.

Yard by yard he explored it, field, hedge, and wood, but little could be discovered, and they moved on. Again the observer halted the machine, and once more it hovered like a hawk seeking its prey. This time his search was rewarded, for at the edge of a wood he saw the flash of a gun. He waited a moment. A second and third flash followed. The battery was located. He signalled his success to the pilot.

Turning to his map, the observer carefully picked out the exact position of the battery, let out his aerial, and proceeded to tap out the wireless emergency call, giving sufficient information to enable every British gun within range to fire on the surprised Huns. A moment later the storm burst. The whole wood and country about seemed to become alive.

Shells shrieked through the air, bursting above the target; others exploded with fearful detonations among the gun emplacements; shrapnel and high explosive, field guns and howitzers combined to erase that particular spot from the face of the earth. Broken trees, clods of turf, shattered guns and human bodies were hurled in the air. Then, as suddenly as the storm started it ceased, but the German battery was wiped out of existence.

The pilot grinned at the observer and pointed towards home. The observer nodded assent. They had accomplished the job they had been sent out to do far more easily than had been expected, and a warm room was better than the damp, chilly air.

At this time they were approximately seven miles over the line, flying low on account of the mist, but for safety's sake the pilot determined to climb to a higher altitude, steering home

78

by compass. It was no good tempting Providence too far, for though the engine was running regularly he knew quite well that a failure had always to be contemplated. In that contingency height might make all the difference between England and Germany.

Then suddenly, as sometimes happens in the air, the fog lifted, and all became clear. In front of him the pilot could see the distant trenches with the canal, beyond which lay home. A moment later "Archie" had picked the machine up—"Bang! Bang! Bang!"—and he was dodging and twisting like a snipe; spinning, zooming, tail-sliding; employing all the tricks of his trade in order to keep clear of those venomous puffs of smoke that appeared dangerously near.

A machine-gun, perched on a housetop, joined in the fray. This was too much; the pilot dived at it, silencing its fire with a burst from the forward gun.

Again he zigzagged for the trenches. Never before did it seem so desirable to cross them; never before had he so clearly noticed how close they ran to the canal.

Then the inevitable happened. A stray fragment from "Archie" struck the engine; the regular explosions stopped, the propeller ceased to revolve. The pilot was too experienced to hope he might hold the machine up long enough to glide over the lines, though he knew that another few hundred yards would have saved them. Instead he looked instinctively for the best place to land, thinking gratefully of his pyjamas and shaving tackle. Similar thoughts seemed to pass through the mind of the observer, judging by the way in which he waved his case at the pilot, while he grinned a sickly smile.

They hit ground about three hundred yards from the canal. They did not land, the surface was too bad, but the observer was thrown clear of the wreckage unharmed. He turned to the help of his companion, who was pinned down under the machine, which had turned on its back. Luckily he too was unhurt, and was soon extricated from the wreckage. Together they looked round, sized up their chances in a minute, then ran hard for the canal, across which lay safety.

Rifle and machine-gun fire opened on them as they bolted, but they reached the canal bank untouched. It was now a matter of seconds. Several Germans were hurrying towards them, and their only hope lay in swimming the canal. Hastily throwing off leather coats and boots they plunged in, striking out for the far side. Half way across they encountered barbed wire, and had to turn back. As they landed the first of the Germans appeared. The chase recommenced. In their haste the enemy had discarded their rifles, probably expecting to find the aviators willing to surrender easily, and as the English officers were sheltered by the canal bank they were protected from fire.

Close by a ruined bridge they again took to the water, this time crossing without hindrance. Two Huns remained on the far side, undecided whether to return from the chase or follow into the water. The appearance of a party of khaki-clad troops decided them, and they dropped into the first available hiding-place—an old barrel amidst the ruins of the bridge. Unfortunately for them their action had been observed, and the barrel was quickly riddled with bullets.

It was a matter of a few minutes for pilot and observer to reach safety, but the day's work was not finished whilst an almost undamaged aeroplane remained in the enemy's hands. Quickly the pilot inquired for the nearest battery, explained the position to the gunners, and a few rounds were fired. Afterwards what remained of the machine could have been packed in a suitcase.

"Curse the blighters, they've made me lose my best pair of silk pyjamas," remarked the pilot.

18

The "Off Pat"

Airmen, like soldiers and sailors, have nicknames for everything; thus the offensive patrol becomes the "Off Pat." This particular type of work gives more opportunities for distinction than almost any other branch of the service, and the large majority of air V.C.s have been won by pilots on the offensive patrol.

One officer set out from an aerodrome near the line on the lookout for hostile aircraft. The morning was misty, and he was unable to fly at any height, so crossed the line at a low altitude, not expecting to encounter a German machine until the fog had cleared. Suddenly, in the way that sometimes happens, he emerged from the haze into clear daylight, and saw above him, coming in his direction, two Hun fighters. Every advantage was theirs. The odds were in their favour, they were flying down wind, and held the best position for manoeuvres.

Then the cunning of the air asserted itself. Swinging his aeroplane round, the British pilot pretended to run from his enemies. The Hun loves a flying foe, probably for the reason that he so rarely sees one, and both machines bore down upon the scout. In their haste neither pilot noticed that the intended prey, though flying slowly, was steadily climbing.

When the foremost fighter was close on his tail and about to open fire, the British pilot swung round the scout, flew under his attacker, zoomed up towards him, and poured in a long burst from the machine-gun. As he passed his enemy he saw the pilot hanging forward limply in his seat, the observer leaning over trying to arouse him, and then down went the nose of the aeroplane plane is was the last effort of a game enemy trying to die with his foe. By inches the British pilot avoided the impending collision, whipped round and dived. Further shots were, however, unnecessary, as the fighter was already falling completely out of control.

Having a few minutes' breathing space the pilot discovered that he had not come off scathless in that last mad rush. His engine had been hit, and, though still running well, was discharging oil, which the wind carried back all over him. Both enemy machines were lying not far apart on the ground below, and as no hostile specks appeared in the sky the pilot descended to make quite sure that the fighters were completely wrecked before returning to his aerodrome.

More excitement was, however, in store for him, for two more Hun aeroplanes arrived on the scene, showing a disposition to attack. This was more than he had bargained for. His engine might give out any minute, he had practically run out of ammunition, and the sights of his machine-gun, as well as himself, were covered with oil.

Thinking that two machines were sufficient bag for one outing, and not wishing to court disaster, he put down the nose of his machine, soon leaving the hostile aircraft far behind, and returned in safety to the aerodrome.

19

To the End

It rarely happens that a German aeroplane stays to fight with several British machines; rather the pilot usually prefers to return to his aerodrome or seek shelter on the ground. Occasionally, however, a Hun of rather more fearlessness than the usual specimen chooses to remain. Sometimes he comes safely through the ordeal, but more usually he pays for his foolhardiness with his life.

On this particular occasion four fighting scouts saw a German fighter a little below them. That the Hun saw the British machines was evident, for he commenced to climb rapidly to gain a position for attack, but before he could accomplish his object the patrol leader gave the signal, and all four scouts dived at the foolhardy fighter which fell to the ground riddled with bullets poured from eight machine-guns—for each aeroplane carried two guns.

This, however, was but a foretaste of what was to come, a mere appetiser before settling down to a glut of fighting. Luckily the patrol leader kept his eyes open, or he would have failed to notice the arrival of four red Albatross scouts riding high amidst the clouds.

Four against four—the latest type of machine of each army. There seemed every prospect of a fight to the death, a gladiatorial display unequalled by any of the combats of the Caesars.

The Germans had the advantage of height, and in their first dive concentrated their fire upon a single British machine, which burst into flames, falling blazing to the earth, before the combat proper had commenced.

Four to three against are heavy odds in the air, and with all seven machines flying at speeds in the neighbourhood of a hundred and twenty miles an hour, formation was soon lost, the air becoming for a time one mass of whirling machines—a regular dogfight.

Out of the mass fell a German scout; one wing collapsed, and the remains fell to join the destroyed British machine.

With the odds even again, the dogfight broke up and three separate duels commenced.

The patrol leaders of either side singled each other out, manoeuvring for position, and reserving their fire until certain of a hit. Round each other they flew, now zooming, then stalling, side-slipping, looping, diving—employing all the tricks of which they were capable. At last the German got his machine into a favourable position; both sights were in line with his foe, and even as he pressed the trigger of his gun the British machine got into a spin, falling rapidly earthwards.

Thinking that he had disposed of his opponent, the German turned to assist his brethren, attacking the nearest British scout before the pilot was aware of his arrival. So intent was he on the fight that he did not notice his late opponent flatten out a few thousand feet below, then climb rapidly to renew the attack. A burst of bullets all around the plane forced him to leave his fresh foe, but as he swung round the machine a second burst of bullets caught him, one pierced his brain, leaving the masterless aeroplane to crash to pieces below.

Then the patrol leader turned to help his comrades.

The odds were in favour of the British now, but even as he arrived to help, one of his machines burst into flames and fell, a blazing wreck.

Each side was running short of ammunition, half the combatants on either side were dead; neither thought of flight. It was a fight to the finish.

As the leader joined again in the fray he glanced at his ammunition—a few more bursts and he would be at the mercy of his enemy. Carefully he husbanded each cartridge, firing short bursts as chances occurred. Out of the corner of his eye he saw his comrade suddenly stall, and a moment later swing round into a position of superiority over his enemy.

Then he had to attend to his own foe, but he felt comforted, for he knew that his companion had sent another Hun out of the fight. He could not resist looking again in that direction, just a brief glance, which showed him a red scout failing with one wing crumpled, and the engine roaring madly towards earth. That glance proved his undoing. His foe seized the chance, bullets flew all round; a stinging pain in the wrist, a useless hand, and a broken control lever told the leader that his time had come.

Vainly he strove to manoeuvre his machine; he was now powerless against the German. Curiously he looked round to see the coming death, when across his sight flashed his sole remaining comrade, steering his machine straight at the Hun. There was no time for clever flying, no time for well-placed bursts of fire. Only one thing could be done, and that he did, crashing straight into the Albatross, giving his life for his friend. Locked together in death the two machines fell to earth.

In a dazed manner the Patrol Leader, sole survivor of the combat, watched their fall, then turned, sick with pain, towards the lines. Waveringly he flew, steering with difficulty, faint with loss of blood. As in a mist he saw the trenches far beneath him, by force of habit shut off his engine. Instinct guided him to an open space, and the wheels touched the ground. Slowly the machine ran to a standstill. He was too dazed to move. At last he heard voices, saw figures about him, then his mind gave out, and he faded away into unconsciousness.

20

In the Face of the Sun

Six scouts flying in formation and looking for trouble. Six of the latest aeroplanes built for speed and general excellence, manned by six of the best pilots of the squadron, each machine armed with two guns, and loaded with ammunition. What more could a pilot ask than to be one of such a company?

The leader of the formation, an old hand, felt confidence in his little flock of machines, and was the match of any three Huns himself. Consequently, when, about 7.30 in the evening he saw a body of nine German scouts below him, he just throttled back his engine, and fell from 14,000 feet like a falcon stooping to its prey.

Before the object of his sudden attack had well realised his presence, a jet of flame burst from the port gun of the attacking aeroplane, and the German machine fell into a vertical spin and crashed to ground.

Before the British pilot had time to feel more than a thrill of elation at his success, two more of the enemy scouts were upon him. He came round in a climbing turn to avoid his aggressors, and pressed the trigger of the starboard gun, hoping to rid himself of one opponent. Instead of the bursts of flame which should have resulted the gun remained mute—jammed.

A few holes appeared in his planes; one shot was very close. The Huns were pressing him hard, but he managed to manoeuvre his other gun into position and ward off the danger for a minute. Still, the odds were two to one—big odds in the air, and his chief hope lay in disabling one enemy, and then being left free to finish the other.

With this object in view he concentrated his fire on a particular machine, hoping to hit a vital spot, when like a flash out of the sky swooped another British scout. A moment later one of the enemy appeared to falter, the planes wavered, and then folded back, and the wreck hurtled to earth as the victor rose again to the attack. The other machine, deeming discretion better than valour, fled. Two to one with the odds on was one thing, but with the odds against it became an entirely different proposition.

During the few minutes' peace which followed the pilot had time to look around him. The rest of his small flock were scattered over the heavens, but they were still five in number, in addition to himself. Of the Germans he could only see five, and one retreating in the distance.

Satisfied, he turned to remedy the jam in his gun which had put him at such a disadvantage.

Whilst thus occupied he failed to observe the approach of another opponent, and it was only the spatter of bullets about the nacelle which caused him to look up and see a machine painted bright red zooming away from him. Again the red scout swooped, and the British pilot had to go down in a spin to throw him off for a second and recover from his surprise.

When the fight commenced he had been at an altitude of only a few thousand feet, as his other combats had caused him to lose height, and during the excitement he had lost his bearings and was not sure of his exact position over the country below.

Before he had time to take his bearings the enemy dived a third time, pulled out of the dive when a collision seemed imminent, and did a zooming turn to get into position for attack again. Not once did the Hun put himself in a position where he could be fired on, and each time he repeated the same manoeuvre, the British pilot meanwhile turning and flying towards the sun in order to keep himself from being hopelessly lost.

The German pilot seemed to realise this, and after his third dive altered his tactics, pulled up in the middle of his dive, and as the British pilot swung round into the face of the sun, dived again, pouring out a murderous fire at his dodging foe.

All this time the British pilot had been watching his opponent and vainly striving to make his second gun work properly. Again the German dived, but this time he was caught at his own game. The British pilot throttled back, and the German swept past, only to zoom into the air again. But he had given the patrol leader the chance he wanted. As the Hun shot upwards, he followed close in his enemy's wake, and for the first time poured out shot after shot from the range of a few feet. The red machine continued upwards; then it lost speed, fell tail foremost, recovered, and finally nosedived to the ground.

By now the pilot was thinking of home; he had already experienced three fights, his companions were scattered and out of sight, and one gun was jammed. Also he was not aware of his position, so he kept on flying west into the face of the setting sun. This course would take him over the trenches, and back to his aerodrome.

But rest was not to be his portion yet. He soon descried a speck swooping on him from above, which speck rapidly resolved itself into another of the pugnacious scouts he had been fighting for over an hour. Well, he was not taken by surprise this time, so the attack had already lost half its effect. He waited until the enemy was nearly on him, then swerved in a climbing circle, got above his foe, dived, and pressed the trigger of his remaining gun—and nothing happened. The second gun had jammed!

There was no other alternative but flight. There was not sufficient altitude for clever manoeuvres, so he shamelessly put down his nose and bolted towards the sun. So close to the ground was he that he rose and fell with the contours, jumping hedges, dodging trees, and all the while his enemy followed above like a falcon chasing a frightened hare, and streams of leaden death poured from the German machine-gun.

Frantically he seized the cocking lever of the nearest gun, and gave a despairing tug. Something clicked; he pressed the trigger, and the gun responded. He had overcome the jam.

Round he swung, the German sheering off to avoid him. From now the game was even. Both pilots were experienced, and the closeness to the ground gave little room for fancy flying. Burst after burst was exchanged, and still the machines were intact. Success seemed to favour neither, then suddenly the fire from the Hun machine ceased. The British pilot saw his enemy grope for fresh ammunition, but none was forthcoming—he had used his last round.

Now the tables were turned, and the chaser fled from the vengeance of the pursued. His very haste for escape proved his undoing, for as he blindly fled towards his aerodrome he forgot the proximity of the ground, and crashed into a broad-limbed tree. His machine crumpled into match-wood, and pieces flew into the air and covered the earth for many yards around.

Once more the British pilot turned and flew into the face of the sun. He did not wish to attract undue attention, and so kept low, following the undulations of hills and valleys. Mile after mile he flew, whilst the sun sank lower and lower. However, now, provided he was not again attacked, his compass would be sufficient guide. And then, just as the red rim touched earth, and rosy beams were reflected on the fleecy clouds above, he was conscious of a noise of cheering, and barely twenty feet above the parapet, he crossed the trenches and realised that he was safe at last.

21

Somewhere in England

Wing Headquarters at home is a very different place from Headquarters overseas. Contrary to general expectation the staff at home is necessarily larger and harder worked, for many hours a day have to be put in to administer the training squadrons and special flights which help to maintain the requisite numbers of pilots to wage the war in the air overseas, and to organise new schemes for the better training of pupils and consequent highly skilled squadrons which go to France or the other fronts.

The Wing Headquarters which I will describe is the headquarters of one of the largest training areas in England, and administers, besides a number of British squadrons, several units of our American allies. Besides the Wing Commander, Wing Adjutant, and Equipment Officer, there are specialists in gunnery, bombing, wireless, photography, aerial fighting, and several other branches, through all of which a pupil must pass before qualifying for his wings.

First, Headquarters itself. It is situated on the edge of a low-lying country town, with its aerodromes some miles away on higher ground. A few months ago it was a mill, but now, in the place of wheat and flour it harbours many officers who work incessantly, and everlastingly try to get posted to an easier job overseas. As befits the place, it is ivy-clad, and a pleasant stream flows through the garden, under the sluices of the mill, and forms a wide pool in front of the house.

Birds twitter in the ivy, rooks quarrel in the tall elms which guard the lawns, and some few trout may be seen in the clear waters of the river. There is also a garden where in springtime snowdrops, aconites, crocuses and anemones bloom, and later in the year warm, juicy pears ripen on the old brick wall.

But it is the stream—and the trout which live in it—which form the chief attraction of the mill. And thereby hangs a tale.

The Wing staff had just moved into the mill from a previous headquarters, and the G.O.C. decided to pay a visit and inspect the new building. In the adjutant's office he noticed several fishing rods on the wall, and, turning to a squadron commander, asked:

"Do you find any difficulty in getting the Wing on the telephone now that they are down here?"

The squadron commander, not noticing the twinkle in the general's eyes, seriously replied:

"Well, perhaps there is a little delay, sir, but I put that down to the fact that they've only just moved, and are not quite straight yet."

"'Umph," said the general, "if I had a trout stream running outside my window you'd never get me on the telephone at all."

Three people fish the pools and vie with each other for the capture of the largest fish, and a long-standing dinner awaits the man who lands "the sergeant-major," a huge, old, hook-nosed bull-trout, who haunts the darkest deepest pool at the back of the mill. Of these three one sings loud the praises of Alaska, and the mighty fish to be caught when the thermometer registers below zero, another upholds the attractions of Sweden and his native Ireland, and the third, who has but recently caught the fishing fever, says little but fishes the hardest of them all. Sometimes a rising fish is sighted, even from the C.O.'s office. Work stops, a waiting rod is taken up, and a few minutes later a plump one-pounder lies gasping in the net.

Dogs, too, abound at the mill. Trojan, the sheepdog, takes precedence of the others, both from his ownership and his dignified mien. This dignity suffers at times when the word "Germans" is spoken near him. Then his sedateness vanishes, and the air re-echoes with his barks, dust flies as he springs at imaginary foes, and the performance ends with a stately bow. An apologetic look comes into his eye, and he once more becomes the dignified guardian of the property. "Wogger," the bulldog, is also a favourite, and the sporting terrier, the spaniel puppy, and even the alleged griffon, take their share of public favour.

Of the staff little need be said. It consists chiefly of "crocks" who are no good for overseas, being "old soldiers, broken in the wars." Thus the E.O. carries his arm in a sling, and the adjutant makes a broken leg an excuse for wearing shoes and slacks, the Wireless Officer pauses for breath every fifty yards, the Flying Examiner periodically hops round on one leg—rumour has it that gout is the cause—and most of the other officers suffer from some ailment. Quite a substantial sum must be drawn by the Wing in pensions and wound gratuities. Yet still they carry on—a ten-or twelve-hour day—and hope for the time when health may be restored and the front line see them again.

When speaking of Headquarters one must not forget the men and women who help to carry on the good work. Little need be said of the men. Like the officers, they have in most cases served overseas, and are no longer fit to carry on abroad. It is the women who most deserve mention, for fully half the staff are members of the W.A.A.C. or Women's Legion. Great was the wailing when male clerks were taken away and women substituted, but with a few N.C.O.s to superintend, the W.A.A.C.s have done splendidly, and office work goes on as smoothly as ever.

Also it has been found that tea can be prepared in a much abler way by a woman than by a heavy-handed orderly, so even if the telephones are rather annoying on occasion, or letters appear with words spelled in new and marvellous ways, we merely smile sadly at the memories of the days before the war, initial the correction, and "carry on."

"Women drivers for the cars!" The look on the face of the flight sergeant when he heard the news was sublime in its resignation. Sadly he thought of his perfect gears and glossy coach-work; reluctantly he saw the last male driver leave for the depot. Then he buckled to, took the women in hand, and in a few days he wore a smiling face, his buttons and boots took a brighter polish, and, marvellous to relate, the cars continued to run.

So one and all, officers, men and women, keep on with the work, and as the papers speak of victories in the air, perhaps sigh softly to themselves, and think of their share of turning out the pilots who are bringing victory daily nearer.

22

The Sunken Road

Spotting for the gunners is not the most pleasant of tasks, and when this is done on an old-fashioned "Quirk" the work becomes at times really objectionable. It had got to the objectionable stage for the pilot and observer, who were aloft signalling the results of shots back to the heavy batteries on this April day. Both of them were thoroughly "fed up." The shooting of the heavies was not good; O.K.s had been few; and "Archie" had been even more of a nuisance than usual. Then the final touch came to their misery, for out of the blue appeared two dots which rapidly resolved themselves into two Halberstadt scouts.

The observer saw them first, and turned round to draw the attention of the pilot to the approaching aeroplanes. That worthy was far too annoyed to smile in the approved manner, but merely turned his machine, and flew straight at the nearest Hun. It was the only thing to do; flight was impossible, and the chances of coming safely out of the unequal combat were very small.

Both scouts charged down upon the slow, cumbersome Quirk, and the end soon came. Hopelessly outmanoeuvred, pilot and observer put up a gallant fight, but their wary enemies gave them no chance, and the British machine put her nose down and fell earthwards, controls shot through, and quite unmanageable. The observer turned in his seat, and held out his hand in mute goodbye. The pilot, realising the utter impossibility of doing anything to stop the downward plunge, sank back in his seat, and waited for the end.

Down came the machine, not diving steeply, but gliding naturally and steadily. Both occupants mentally judged the exact spot where the crash would happen, and both prayed to escape the torture of fire. It did not occur to either to climb over and drop, exchanging the slow agony of minutes for the almost instantaneous death. Perhaps some prescience warned them that the faintest hope still existed, and the young die hard; so they both sat and waited.

Eventually the aeroplane crashed approximately where they had both estimated it would reach earth, and they were shot clear of the wreckage unhurt. A few bruises and a cut over the observer's eye, caused by his being thrown through the upper plane, were the extent of the damage.

"Lie still," shouted the pilot.

He saw the Halberstadts hovering over-head, and realised that any movement would cause machine-gun fire to open on them. Down came one of the scouts to within a few hundred feet of the ground to make sure of the end of the British airmen. It circled low, and the pilot evidently saw the motionless bodies, and, satisfied as to the end of the fight, mounted in quick circles, and rejoined his waiting comrade. A few minutes later both machines vanished in the distance, and pilot and observer got up and looked around them.

The Quirk was damaged beyond repair, undercarriage, planes and fuselage were wrecked, and the engine lay half buried in the ground. Little remained undamaged except the machine-guns, which they removed, together with some drums of ammunition. They then looked around for shelter. The wreck lay in a large field near a hedge, on the far side of which ran a seemingly little-used sunken road. As far as they could judge they were about ten miles over the line, and not close to any large town.

Before deciding on a course of action they sought shelter in the sunken road, to escape possible observation by any of the enemy who chanced that way. The observer carried a compass on his wrist, and they easily located their position on the maps taken from the machine, and determined to try and reach their own lines under cover of the night.

Shortly after making this decision they heard voices, and through the hedge observed a party of eight German mechanics approaching the wrecked Quirk. Evidently the victorious pilot had returned to the aerodrome and reported his success, and the men had been sent out to salve the damaged aeroplane.

Not a minute was to be lost. Placing their machine-guns in position, both pilot and observer waited the opportunity, and then two leaden streams poured into the approaching party. Several dropped at once; the rest scattered and took shelter or lost themselves to view as speedily as possible.

Having revealed their position, both Englishmen realised that their only safety lay in rapid flight; so both guns were damaged and put out of action, and they went speedily down the sunken road.

Some miles farther on the road entered a wood, which at that time of year—April—offered excellent cover, and induced them to leave the lane which had sheltered them so far. A disused gravel pit promised excellent hiding, and they decided to wait here until nightfall, taking it in turn to watch from the branches of a tree which grew at the edge of the pit.

First watch fell to the pilot, and he soon ascended the trunk and proceeded to look about him. Owing to his elevation, he could see over a large tract of the surrounding country. Some few miles off he saw an aerodrome, evidently the one from which the Halberstadts had ascended, and from which came the mechanics who had caused them to leave the sunken road. As his gaze travelled round he saw the huts of an encampment and a railway passing beside it. He carefully noted the positions of these on his map, and then his eyes rested on the country close at hand. He seemed near the centre of a fairly large wood, and as far as he could perceive the solitude was undisturbed. Presently he noticed a darker patch among the fresh green of the budding trees, a patch he was unable to account for, and which aroused his curiosity.

Descending the tree, he called his companion, and together

they went cautiously towards the spot. No sign of life was to be seen, all was still. Carefully they crept forward until the planes and fuselage of a biplane were clearly discernible, caught in the branches overhead. By the markings it was a British machine, a type new to the country—the latest artillery aeroplane sent to France.

A very few minutes sufficed to take the observer up one of the trees to inspect the wrecked biplane, and his cry of horror advised the waiting pilot of what he saw. Pilot and observer of the machine were both dead; one shot through the head, the other through the heart. The aeroplane, bereft of guiding hands, had fallen into the wood, and remained suspended in the branches of the ancient trees.

Not wishing to give away their own position again, the British airmen determined to wait until nightfall before taking any action. Then petrol was taken from the half-empty tank, and a match was applied to the inflammable fabric, and in a few seconds the whole construction became a mass of flames—a fit funeral pyre for the men who had perished with her.

Pilot and observer left hurriedly in the direction of the lines.

Some three hours later they found themselves nearing the support trenches, and had to proceed more warily. Little by little they crept forward until the front line was reached. Here all was quiet, but it would need some ingenuity to cross the line and pass the wire before reaching "No Man's Land" and home. Also, in addition to the danger from the Germans, there was the possibility of getting shot when entering the British lines.

For a long while they lay silently behind the German parados, hoping that a way of escape would present itself, when suddenly the night became full of noise of bursting bombs and gleaming bayonets, and dimly seen khaki-clad figures leaped down into the German trenches.

Seizing their opportunity, both pilot and observer ran for safety. Luck guided them to the gaps in the wire, and in a few minutes they fell into British trenches, and realised that their good fate had held, and that they had not been saved from a crashed machine to languish in a German prison.

23

Airmen of the Sea

Few people realise the variety of types of airships we now possess, or the multiplicity of uses to which they are put. Apart from the "Blimps" which are often seen over London, or at coastal towns, there are also now in use other airships.

The chief uses to which these airships are put are reconnaissance and submarine chasing.

Reconnaissance airships operate from their bases over many miles of sea, constantly on the lookout for the German fleet to appear, in order that news of its appearance may be signalled to the British ships. British airships played an important part in the battle of Jutland, and it is safe to assume that a still bigger role will be played on the day when the German fleet again leaves its harbours for the open sea.

Not a destroyer leaves the Heligoland Bight or the bolt-holes of Ostend and Zeebrugge without being seen by our waiting airships, unless the movements are carried out in fog or under cover of darkness. When the papers report that returning destroyers were intercepted by our light forces one may be certain that the wireless messages tapped from our airships many thousand feet in the air have been the means of conveying sufficient information to the fleet to enable the admiral to send vessels to the right spot and intercept the returning raiders.

It is, however, on the submarine patrol that the airship shows up to the greatest advantage. From his height, poised some thousands of feet above the sea, the pilot can see any signs of movement for many miles around. Not only can he scan the surface, but masses several fathoms deep can be discerned from above.

Once a submarine is sighted the chase begins. With its superior speed the airship rapidly overhauls the U-boat whose every turn and twist are visible. If the vessel is still on the surface a few well directed bombs will be sufficient to put it out of action, and the airship continues its patrol.

Should the submarine have time to submerge conditions are different, and if it is more than a few feet underwater bombs are useless. Under these conditions the airship descends and sinks a depth charge near the submerged U-boat. A muffled roar, a huge column of water, and presently a growing patch of oil on the surface show that the charge has taken effect, severely shaking the submarine, starting the plates, upsetting its equilibrium, and causing it to sink slowly to the bed of the sea, where it is likely to remain.

It must not be supposed that a submarine always seeks safety by flight or that airship crews are immune from danger. On many occasions the anti-aircraft gun on board the U-boat is got into action, machine-guns are trained on the dirigible, and the pilot has all his work cut out to steer safely through the storm. An airship is a large target, and, needless to say, has not the manoeuvring powers of an aeroplane. Should she manage to get into the correct position to drop her bombs the submarine will probably come off worse in the encounter, but sometimes a well directed shot may ignite the gas-bag or damage the engine of the dirigible, and the remains plunge down into the sea. The airship becomes overdue, and at last the crew are posted as missing.

Nor is this the only danger to be encountered. Sometimes sudden storms arise many miles from land, against which the airship is powerless to make headway. The whole structure may be wrecked in the sea, and the crew drowned, or petrol give out, and the airship drift at the mercy of the wind until the crew are able to descend, many miles from any sign of land and far out of the track of vessels.

Notwithstanding these hardships, cheerfully endured, the airship groups of the Royal Air Force carry on their work of reconnaissance and the destruction of submarines. It is safe to say that a large proportion of enemy submarines destroyed fall to the credit of this arm of the air.

24

"Six Machines went out"— (harassing the enemy)

When aeroplanes are sent out to "harass the enemy," as the official *communiqués* put it, it is fairly certain that the pilots will have good tales to tell on their return.

Officers are sent out with no definite orders; their sole object is to annoy the Hun as much as possible, destroy his stores, damage his communications and demoralise his personnel to the greatest extent. Generally the pilots concerned manage to give a good account of themselves on their return, and rarely does an officer state that he has "nothing to report."

Six machines of a certain squadron went out to carry on the good work. One pilot returned with no special feat to his credit, another with a failing engine. All the others had tales to tell.

One pilot crossed the trenches at an immense height, dodging "Archie," and keeping in the clouds until he was well over the lines. He then throttled back his engine, planed down to a much lower altitude, and looked for a chance to "harass the enemy."

Chances are plentiful in the air, and he soon observed a concentration of troops near a station, soldiers evidently just going up into the line. Two bombs dropped from five hundred feet in the densest part of the mass caused the enemy to scatter, leaving several motionless bodies on the road. Following up this with a brisk fire from his machine-gun, the pilot obtained several more hits, and, having completely disorganised the whole parade, delaying their entrainment and thereby causing much anxiety in the hard-pressed front line, he departed from the vicinity before it became too hot for him.

A little later he saw a battery of guns in action, and did his share towards helping the infantry who were suffering the bombardment in the trenches by diving to within a hundred feet of the ground and driving the gunners from their guns.

His next item was more in the recognised line of the air. Having climbed to a height of some thousands of feet, he saw below him a British machine trying to register a battery on to an invisible target, at the same time fighting off an attacking Hun. A dive through the air, a long burst from the Vickers gun, and the Hun departed for home, crippled and badly frightened, while the British two-seater carried on its work undisturbed.

This completed the first pilot's work, for his petrol was running short, so he returned to his aerodrome to see what the others had done.

He found two pilots had returned, in addition to the one with the failing engine. Of these one had little to report beyond having fired all his ammunition at troops in the support trenches, but the other had enjoyed quite an exciting flight.

Shortly after crossing the trenches, where he fired a few shots just to see if his gun was working well, he espied infantry on the march, dropped a couple of bombs on the column and dived, firing with his machine-gun at the flying troops.

He then noticed a large enemy two-seater, which fled at his approach, but was rapidly overhauled, and forced to fight.

The combat was short and decisive. Hopelessly outclassed, the Hun went down in a spin, crashing in the trenches.

During the fight the British machine had descended to within a few hundred feet of the ground, and seeing that certain shell-holes in No Man's Land were packed with Germans awaiting the signal to attack, the pilot dived at them, flying up and down between the lines, pouring a murderous fire into the shell-holes, quite undisturbed by the fusillade of rifle and machine-gun fire which was directed at him from the trenches. Having at last expended all his ammunition he was forced to return to the aerodrome.

A third pilot who returned whilst the first arrivals were discussing the day's work had encountered bad luck. Soon after crossing the trenches his petrol tank had been pierced by a stray bullet, and with a failing engine he had struggled back home, where he obtained another machine and again set out.

A similar thing occurred on his second trip, but this time he could not reach the aerodrome, landing just short of it, unharmed. Thinking it was not wise to tempt Providence too far, he did not venture out again.

The last pilot to return limped home across the sky like a badly winged duck, steering erratically, with an aileron flapping and engine rattling like a tank. He flopped down upon the aerodrome, the machine collapsing as soon as earth was reached. Out of the wreckage scrambled the pilot, unhurt and cheery.

"Nasty mess," he exclaimed. "The old bus had done nearly fifty hours too."

Inquiries elicited the information that he had flown over the countryside, firing at any troops he had seen, until he espied a collection of huts which aroused his curiosity.

Planing low he had dropped two bombs. The resulting explosion surpassed all expectations. Huts seemed to leap bodily into the air, a sheet of flame spurted up a hundred feet, and a dense pall of black smoke spread over the wreckage. Before this cleared away a violent fire from hidden "Archies" burst around the aeroplane.

So thickly was the air plastered with shells that dodging was out of the question. The pilot put down the nose of his machine, and went all out. How often he was hit he did not realise until at last he got out of range, when he found that his rudder controls were cut, one aileron broken and flapping, whilst splintered ribs peered through the torn planes and loose wires whistled in the air.

Despite the knocking, rattling engine, he had crept home,

steering rudely by means of one aileron, crossed the lines and reached the aerodrome unhurt.

And that is the account of six machines which went out to harass the enemy.

25

An Interlude

Brains and quickness of thought are as necessary to the airman as pluck, endurance and skill, in aerial manoeuvres.

The pilot of a single-seater fighter of the latest type, whilst cruising far over the lines, saw below him three slow, old-fashioned enemy machines, flying steadily westwards, as though to cross the lines into British territory.

Unfortunately the Huns were too far off to be attacked, and should his presence be realised he knew quite well that they would fly for home and safety long before he was within range. He therefore flew up into the clouds, and then turned in the direction in which the enemy machines were going.

Judging his time, he pushed down the nose of his machine, dived out of the cloud to the Huns beneath, and, when close enough to be sure of his mark, pressed the trigger of his gun. A stream of lead played about the German machines, but none of them returned the fire.

Once before the pilot had heard of a similar occurrence. This flashed through his mind, and pulling back the control lever, he "zoomed" up again into the cloud.

He was only just in time, for as he vanished into the vapour three enemy scouts appeared. The slow machines were the bait, and the English aeroplane was the expected prey, for the pilot was well known and feared by the Germans in that part of the line.

Once he knew the odds against him he no longer hesitated.

Down once more, through the clouds he came, straight at the nearest scout. A short burst from his gun and the hostile machine wavered, then slowly fell into a spin, hurtling downwards and crashing far below.

The odds were still five to one. True, three of the enemy machines were slow and old-fashioned, and taken alone might have been accounted for one by one, but an addition of two fast-flying scouts manoeuvred by skilful pilots gave the matter an entirely different aspect.

The British pilot did not wait. No sooner had one machine been accounted for than he flew at the next, banking, zooming, side-slipping, ever trying to reach the spot from which his enemy was most vulnerable. All the time the other scout was trying to secure a favourable position to fire at the attacking fighter, and the three old two-seaters were firing long-range bursts as opportunity afforded.

For some minutes this competition for position continued, each party firing short bursts without definite results, and then suddenly the deciding factor arrived.

Out of the sky loomed a two-seater British fighter of the latest type. It was just proceeding on a special job, but before the enemy had realised its arrival the new pilot steered his machine into the dog-fight. A long burst from the rear gun caused one of the Hun fighters to stagger in its flight, then drop its nose and leave the combat. Evidently the pilot was badly hit.

Then together the two British machines charged the German scouts. A short affair ensued before both Huns thought discretion the better part of valour, put their machines into spins to evade their adversaries' fire, and fled for home.

Meanwhile the other two machines had vanished in the clouds, so the British pilots, seeing no more immediate work before them, separated and returned to their jobs.

26

Four Hours of Life

The sun was well up, and the air was beginning to recover from the effects of a cold night as the pilot walked into the hangar. Mechanics were already busy about his machine, a two-seated fighter of the latest type, and he watched the final touches put to a few patches in the planes, which covered the holes gained in a combat on the previous day. Then the aeroplane was wheeled out into the sunlight, petrol and oil tanks were filled, drums of ammunition were brought for the guns, and the pilot took his seat to test the engine. He left nothing to chance or his mechanics. Already his name was feared by the enemy, and few Germans waited to inquire too closely into the movements of the well-known fighter.

At the sound of the engine an observer approached hurriedly, fearing to keep the pilot waiting. He climbed into the cockpit, fingered his gun, and arranged the maps.

When the pilot looked round inquiringly he nodded assurance; they had made their plans previously, and each knew that the other could be relied upon to do his share of the business.

With a roar from the engine the aeroplane left the ground, and headed for the lines. The pilot glanced at his watch; it needed a few minutes to 10 o'clock, and he hoped to be over enemy territory by half-past. Steadily eastwards he flew, the machine gaining altitude the while. Slowly the needle of the aneroid crept round the dial. Five thousand, ten thousand, twelve thousand, higher and higher they climbed, and colder grew the atmosphere. Even on that springlike day it was cold at twelve thousand feet, and the heat thrown back from the engine was comforting to the officers behind it. At twelve thousand feet the trenches were visible ahead—serried, tangled lines amidst the shell-torn country. About 10.30 No Man's Land was crossed at an altitude of over sixteen thousand feet, and both pilot and observer prepared for business.

A few minutes later, the observer, whilst looking behind for any signs of activity, felt the machine rock from side to side. It was the pilot's signal, and following that worthy's pointing hand he saw a large German machine gaining height ahead of them.

The combat was of short duration. The superior powers of the British aeroplane enabled the pilot to obtain his favourite place under the tail of the enemy. From this position he fired a long burst from both guns, and the German machine fell into a nose dive. A moment later all four planes collapsed, and the wreckage fell thousands of feet to the ground below.

The hands of the clock marked 10.40.

After replacing the partly-used drum of ammunition the pilot looked around him. Several enemy machines were in sight, but none dared attack. The British machine was well known, and the German pilots had probably witnessed the combat which had just ended fatally for one of their band.

A little below and not far off was a Hun apparently working for the artillery. Down went the nose of the fighter, and at about a hundred yards' range jets of flames poured from the muzzles of both forward guns. For a moment the doomed enemy wavered, unable to reply, and incapable of fleeing from its faster adversary. Then the whole fabric seemed to burst into flames, pieces of the shot-about planes and fuselage broke off, and the remains dropped like a stone.

The hands of the clock marked 10.50.

As the pilot paused for breath after the terrific dive, the crackle of machine-gun fire broke on his ears, and he swung the aeroplane round to face his foe. For a moment the enemy was in the arc of fire, and a burst was fired from close quarters before he swerved out of range. Then the observer's turn came, and he pumped lead from his gun until water poured in a stream from the radiator of the German engine, and the Hun pushed down the nose of his machine and fled.

But the British aeroplane had not come off scathless this time. A slight hit in the radiator caused a leak, the water from which froze on the windscreen, partially obscuring the pilot's view. Also one of the elevators was damaged, so altogether the pilot thought it better to return to his aerodrome before further harm was done. Accordingly he banked his aeroplane, swung round, and a few minutes later crossed the lines.

His homeward journey, however, was not destined to be uneventful, and before reaching the aerodrome he encountered a German machine of the type first destroyed. Another short combat ensued, and the enemy aeroplane went down in a steep spiral, emitting smoke. Close to the ground it burst into flames, and crashed in the British lines.

The time was 11.15.

A very few minutes sufficed to take them home. The pilot landed, inspected the damage, and realising that the aeroplane could not be made serviceable in a few minutes, obtained another machine. Whilst this was being prepared, he and his observer stood by smoking—hardly a word was spoken as to their four combats.

At 11.45 they left the aerodrome again, and half an hour later were in their old position on the other side of the lines. They had not long to wait before a hostile aircraft was seen, for the Germans seemed exceptionally busy that day, and once more the pilot opened the throttle of the engine and the fighter raced after the already fleeing foe. This time, however, a more experienced airman had to be dealt with, for as the British machine got into position, the German swung round and fired wildly at his enemy.

Unfortunately for him his aeroplane was not good enough, and after a short period of manoeuvring the English pilot was able to fire a burst from one of his guns, and the stricken machine broke into pieces as it fell vertically to the ground.

The pilot looked about him, and seeing no more hostile aer-oplanes, thought of lunch. He looked round at his observer, and made unmistakable signs. The observer cast his eyes around the sky, and then signified assent.

They landed at 1.20.

27

A Narrow Margin

Whilst, generally speaking, the work of the Kite-Balloon Section of the Royal Air Force is not so full of excitement as that of the aeroplane branches, occasionally the observers have a day in every way as exciting as those experienced by their more mobile brethren of the air.

On one particular day an ascent was to be made by a single observer who had instructions to seek out a particular battery and range some "heavies" on to the German guns.

The observer duly fastened the webbing which attached him to his parachute, counted his binoculars, maps, pencils and other necessary instruments, entered the wicker basket slung from the deformed sausage above him, and rapidly shot up into the air as the cable unwound from the huge winch below. Gradually the speed of his ascent slackened as the altitude grew, until the balloon stopped some thousands of feet above the ground.

The wind blew in the direction of the trenches some three miles away, and the basket heeled over in the breeze.

After looking around him and taking his bearings thoroughly, the observer proceeded to inspect his map and identify the exact position of the hostile battery. This found, he signalled to the waiting "heavies," and watched for the first shot. A minute later he observed a burst of smoke some hundred yards short of the target. Quickly the correction was signalled to those below, and a second puff appeared a few yards beyond the gun-emplacements. The third shot was a direct hit, and he sent the signal for battery fire to be opened. Immediately the air was filled with smoke from the bursting shells, clouds of dust arose from the ground around the stricken battery, and flashes of fire pierced the darkness. Then a period of quiet followed, during which time the air slowly cleared, and then the result of the bombardment was seen. Most of the guns were disabled, their crews were dead or wounded, the gun-pits were destroyed. The observer gleefully sent down the message to cease fire, and looked about him for another target on which to range the "heavies."

It was not long before he perceived flashes which betrayed the position of more German guns, and a message soon reached the British battery giving their exact position on the map. The sighting shots were fired, and general battery fire was about to commence when out of the clouds appeared a speck which resolved itself into a red Albatross scout.

Quickly the observer sent down the final corrections, before the hostile machine came within range, and "Archie" opened fire. Dots of cotton-wool like smoke covered the sky above, below and around the German scout, but the pilot treated these manifestations of anger with contempt, and proceeded on his way towards the helpless balloon. The observer glanced around him for help. He was loath to signal to be pulled down, but unless a lucky shot from "Archie" ended the career of the attacking machine or a British aeroplane appeared on the scene it seemed that he was in for a very thin time.

When about fifty yards from the balloon the scout dived, opened a burst of fire with incendiary bullets, and charged straight at the envelope. Either his shots went wide in his haste or the bullets failed to set the gas alight, for nothing happened, and the pilot zoomed up over the observer and wheeled preparatory to another attack.

Meanwhile the observer stood helpless in his basket. He had no means of replying to the German's fire; the anti-aircraft batteries had ceased shelling owing to the danger of hitting the kite-balloon, and his only hope lay in the quick arrival of a British aeroplane. Nothing happened, and as the balloon strained at the cable before the wind, the scout banked and charged again at its foe.

Then the observer decided that the time to act had come. He signalled to those below, and immediately the structure commenced to descend. He was, however, too late in his decision, for a burst of bullets from a range of about thirty yards found their mark, and with a roar, the gas-bag burst into flames and began to fall earthwards.

The observer knew that one source of safety remained to him, and he took it. Like a flash he climbed over the edge of the basket and dropped into space. For a moment his body whistled through the air after the parachute had been torn from its sheath outside the basket; then the envelope opened, his descent slackened, and he commenced to drop gently downwards. The blazing envelope fell to earth in flames, and as he felt the heat as it passed within a few yards of him, he thanked the powers that he had jumped in time.

His descent was not destined to be without excitement. The German pilot, having accounted for the balloon, now turned to attack its late occupant. Passing within a few yards of the slowly-drifting officer the Hun opened fire. Bullets whistled through the air around the observer, but none touched him, and as the scout wheeled to make another attack relief appeared.

Out of the sky appeared the avenger—a tiny machine bearing the welcome red, white and blue rings. Straight at the Hun it dived, the pilot reserving his fire until sure of his mark. Balloons were the German's prey, not fighting aeroplanes, and the Hun turned and fled. Unfortunately for him the British scout was the faster, and he was soon overhauled and forced to fight.

At the first burst the Hun appeared to be in difficulties. Either he was hit and unable to control his machine or he lost his head in the danger. Whatever happened he presented an absolute "sitter" to the British pilot, who dived to within a few yards and poured in a terrific stream of lead. The German machine appeared to burst into fragments, the planes falling to earth apart from the fuselage, the petrol tank becoming a roaring mass of fire.

Meanwhile the observer was drifting before the wind towards the German lines. He was dropping rapidly, but in his state of helplessness the seconds seemed minutes, and the trenches grew rapidly closer and closer. For one moment he forgot his helplessness as the blazing wreck of his late adversary passed him on its plunge to earth. Then the fear of landing returned to him. Would he reach earth before he crossed the trenches? Would he land to find himself welcomed in safety by khaki-clad friends or would he be captured by foes in field-grey?

Every second he fell closer to earth, and every second the wind seemed to grow in strength as it wafted him to the enemy. Little by little, foot by foot, he crept closer to the trenches. He could see the upturned faces watching his progress. He could see the action of the enemy as they raised rifles which spurted forth the leaden messengers of death at him. So occupied was he in watching, fascinated with the apprehension of death, that he failed to notice his closeness to earth, failed to realise that the parapet was below him, until he was brought to his senses with the jerk of landing.

Too dazed to move, he stood on the parapet. He could not realise that his descent was over, and that he was within an ace of safety. A blinding flash and a deafening roar brought him to his senses. Luckily he was not hit, as the bomb fell short, but he was aroused to the sense of immediate danger, and threw himself backwards into the British trench as the fire of a machine-gun swept over the spot where he had stood a moment before.

28

The Aerial Mail, 1921

It was just getting dark, and the pilot smiled as he climbed into his machine. He was muffled in furs and shivering with the cold of the northern climate, but he was due south, bound for India on his bi-weekly mail trip, and the thought of the sunny land he was visiting cheered him up.

There were three of them on this route, one of the most popular amongst the G.P.O. pilots, but he was the new-comer, and this was his first trip. He had previously been on the Atlantic route—monotonous journeys backwards and forwards to America—and had not seen many strange lands, though travel was easy and fast since the close of the Great War.

"All the mails on board?" he asked.

He was answered in the affirmative, but glanced down at the huge receptacles slung from the bottom planes to see that all was in order. The machine's carrying capacity was about ten tons, but as he had to land at Malta and Suez to gather fresh bags of letters, the aeroplane was so far carrying only half its load. All seemed well, and he signalled to the waiting mechanic:

"Contact."

A moment later the two huge propellers commenced to revolve quietly, the explosions of the engines being hardly audible, so well did the silencers do their work.

For a while after the Great War the noise from the sky had grown greater and greater as larger numbers of aeroplanes were used, but at last a law was passed making the provision of silenc-

116

ers a necessity, thus obtaining peace for the dwellers on earth without the resultant loss of power always previously feared by aviators.

Waving his hand to the little knot of spectators who always assembled to see the departure of the mail, the pilot moved forward the throttle control, gently pulled back the elevator, causing the machine to rise straight from the ground at a steep angle, and soon disappear from sight in the clouds and the gathering dusk.

When the fifteen thousand feet level was reached, the pilot set his course preparatory to turning in for the night. It was getting darker, and down below, through a gap in the clouds, he distinguished the lights of Paris. The first stage took approximately ten hours, and he counted on sleeping till dawn. In the middle of the fuselage, just behind the planes, was a tiny cubicle, just large enough for a camp bed. Into this he tumbled, and soon fell asleep.

Should an engine stop—a remote contingency—the other would enable the machine to carry on at a reduced speed; and in the event of both motors giving out, the aeroplane would find her own gliding angle and commence to descend, a bell meanwhile ringing loudly in the ear of the pilot, who would have ample time to reach the controls, selecting a landing-place before the machine was near the ground. Should the country prove impossible for an ordinary landing, he could switch on the electric helicopter and settle lightly after a perpendicular descent—a prolonged "pancake" of the old days.

When the pilot awoke he looked down, seeing the deep blue of the Mediterranean all below him. Glancing at his chronometer, he calculated that another hour and a half would take him to Malta, ready for breakfast, before proceeding on his journey. He opened a thermos flask and felt unmistakably hungry.

A little later a smudge appeared on the horizon, then another. The pilot decided that this was Malta, with its sister islands, and seated himself at the controls, putting down the nose of the machine, and throttling back the engine. He picked up the G.P.O.

landing-ground whilst at about five thousand feet, and landed gently. His aeroplane was taken over by the waiting mechanics before he departed to obtain some breakfast.

Whilst he was away the consignment of fresh mails was packed into the receptacle under the planes. Short distance services brought small parcels of post to these large stations from the surrounding country, and took away the bags left by the long-distance machines. Very few towns were without the aerial post, for it was only the remote rural districts which were still supplied by motor transport. The sending of mails by trains had been discontinued long ago, this method of travel being now used only for bulky packages of goods.

When the fuel and oil tanks had been replenished, the bags of letters secured, and the machine looked over, the pilot reappeared, climbed to his seat, leaving for the second, the shortest, stage of his journey. He expected to be in Suez in time to dine, after taking the hour's physical exercise laid down for all Government airmen.

Below him sparkled the fresh blue of the sea, the sun shone warmly on him, well sheltered in the covered cabin. He could see far beneath the huge liners ploughing their ways in well-defined tracks, loaded with merchandise and carrying some few passengers of the poorer class. Far away on his left he could dimly discern faint smudges on the horizon, which he judged to be the hills of Greece. He gazed ahead, looking for the first glimpse of the mysterious African coast.

As he stood he glanced at his instrument board, noticing that one engine was not giving her full revolutions. He walked along the gangway to ascertain the cause of trouble, but, unable to see any defect, decided to stop the engine and investigate. Running on one engine materially decreased the speed of the aeroplane, but he quickly found and rectified the fault, switched on again, and opened up both throttles. He next proceeded to lunch off the food which had been provided at Malta; then settled down to read whilst the machine hurtled through the air.

About five in the evening he sighted the coast of Africa, soon after picking out the mouths of the Nile and the Delta. Straight over Alexandria he steered, leaving Cairo on the right, picking out Suez at the head of the gulf. Even at ten thousand feet the air was appreciably warmer than when over the sea, but it was not until he climbed out of the aeroplane that he fully realised the higher temperature of the land he had reached since yesterday.

An hour a day had to be set aside for physical exercise, so the airman took himself to the tennis courts for a while before arranging for dinner, afterwards returning to the Bellair Hotel.

Whilst dining he received orders to report to the Senior Naval Officer as early as possible. Wondering what this order might mean, he set out for Port Tewfik. There he was introduced to the cause of the order—a King's Messenger who had urgent reasons for wishing to reach Delhi quickly. King's Messengers were the only passengers allowed to travel with the aerial mail, and the pilot welcomed a companion to break the monotony of the journey.

Both men sat up talking far into the night, hung midway between heaven and earth, whilst the aeroplane flew on undisturbed beneath the stars. As the tiny cabin would only hold one, they agreed to take the bed for five hours apiece, for this last stage was a long one. Day broke as the pilot turned in, the rising sun turning the sea to the colour of blood. No land was in sight; the ships far below were the only signs of life.

There was little fear of a forced landing, but in the unlikely event of both engines giving out, forcing the pilot to descend upon the water, the floats would keep the machine riding safely on any but a rough sea, whilst help would soon arrive in answer to the pilot's wireless telephone conversation with the nearest repair ship, of which several were stationed along all long-sea routes.

Once before the pilot had called for help, far out in the Atlantic, and within an hour a speedy motor boat with a crew of mechanics arrived, repaired the engine, and enabled him to continue the voyage.

Some hours later the pilot was aroused by his passenger, who pointed to a line on the horizon showing land ahead. Already a faint smell of the tropics was ascending, the scent growing more pronounced as the aeroplane crossed the coast, steering for its destination.

Below, in place of the monotonous sea, could be seen far-spreading forests, close-packed, white-roofed towns, and the tree-clad slopes of the hills. Later the scene grew less interesting, more forests and fewer towns being visible.

As the sun commenced to decline, far-famed Delhi appeared in sight, the aeroplane dropped earthwards and settled—the journey was ended.

Pilot and passenger got out. The latter left to deliver his dispatches, and the former, after receiving a receipt for the bags of mails he had delivered, departed to enjoy three days' holiday in the new land before returning laden with mails for home.